T0115062

THE BOY
IN THE
ORCHARD

A POEM AND OTHER WRITINGS

ROBERT BERTRAND

Trafford rev. 01/22/2013

 www.trafford.com

North America & international
toll-free: 1 888 232 4444 (USA & Canada)
phone: 250 383 6864 ♦ fax: 812 355 4082

FOREWORD

My mother was a lady, in whose company I found extreme joy and great pleasure. She retained a healthy sense of humor long into old age. A factory worker for many years, she provided for her family of five sons well enough. My father's endeavors caused more "output" than "income". Through the years of caring for the elderly in the family, and heartache in tragedies, Mama was able to find a degree of happiness, even laughter, until her death at ninety-three.

Being able to laugh while dealing with sorrows is a gift; one which I observed with interest and admiration. My brothers and I left one by one, making our ways in life. I am not sure I made my way . . . perhaps I just slowly drifted in directions unclear to me: bewildered, confused, and totally unaware of what the world (or even God) expected of me. I grabbed at whatever straw floated near enough for my hands to reach. However, steadfast in stored memories of my mother's few words of advice, was a bit of magic which floated with me in my bubble, which never burst, and which retained always the magic of her words, "You can do anything you want to do!". One of my brothers remarked once, either in accusation or praise, "You have always done exactly what you wanted to do!" The magic in my mama's voice is what has carried me through life, through every experience, even when I did not even realize that I was doing something, experiencing something that I did not know was something worthless, or extraordinary! Her one statement overshadowed every "put-down" (and there were many) that my father ever said to me. Mama's early guidance to me gave me reason to know that in my heart was a power to reach whatever goals I saw ahead of myself. However long it might be that I am allowed to be on God's green earth, lying on the grass before lying under it, my mama's influence will live on. Here, I have to say that it is rather remarkable that my daughters have lifted in me the confidences left by my mother . . . , or that maybe I have hoisted and passed on to them the same qualities: self confidence; self discipline; self-determination; self-actualization.

It is hoped, even prayerfully expected, that every parent will care for, provide for, teach, discipline and set excellent examples for their offspring (and other young ones in their charge). When an aging parent, grandparent, old aunt or uncle, or any non-related older neighbor has need of assistance, it would be considered a blessing to be the one who can be there for the ones in need.

Looking back in time, face to face with life, it can be difficult at times to see clearly whether I have done right by the people (young or old) who were around me. The guidance and attention which I tried to give in a proper manner can be fuzzy in a memory growing dimmer as time passes. Memories can be like a lovely piece of lace, beautifully designed, expertly stitched with threads in exactly the right places, leaving open spaces (holes in a piece of memory); empty spaces which are as important in the "doily" of life that are as important as the artistically knitted threads. Like in a Chinese painting, the open, blank spaces are as important to the composition of life as the painted spaces. And so it is with life's memories. It is important to remember that there are open spaces which are like those in a beautiful piece of lace.

On looking back, remembering events from my past, I can wish that I had done more, done differently, done less. Sometimes regret creeps in quietly (which I am quick to murder) and I wonder why I chose certain words to speak, or why I spoke at all. Just as often, I think of times when I should have, but did not, speak up or act on another person's behalf. I once wrote a poem entitled, "Words Never Spoken": Those are the ones which haunt me most, and are the most hurtful. Those can cause crushing heartache, guilt with every heartbeat, confusion crawling through my brain . . . all because I did

NOT say something, or DO something befitting the circumstances. Stupid, selfish, unwise, insensitive: all descriptive adjectives to which most of us can relate. Who hurt more? Who cried the most? The one I didn't defend? The one I offended? Or myself?

Memories of events vividly remain, while the circumstances controlling the events of the time are like the open spaces in the doily. If the memory is sweet, beautiful, a treasured one, then it is like a lovely piece of lace. If it is a regrettable experience, it is more like a piece of old rag, tattered and torn, full of patches from years of trying to figure out why . . . . Once when my daughter, Elizabeth, and I were walking the back streets of Paris, France, we saw on the sidewalk an old tattered silk scarf. It was faded, dirty and battered, but the flowers were still colorful and quite beautiful. We picked it up, washed it gently, and for years I have kept it, because of the mystery, the history, the wondering and the imagining of its story. To whom did it belong? Why was it left lying there? How did she lose it? Was she pretty? What was she like? I have never written a story about the scarf, nor la dame who might have lost it, or tossed it away for some reason. I am sure there is a story there. There are stories everywhere and with everyone one meets. I seldom write about myself, but I have met many people who have stories to tell and for some reason they seem to want to tell them to me. I enjoy writing about them, as I have done in this book.

THE BOY IN THE ORCHARD

I stand in the mist amidst an orchard where the scent
Of ripening, withering, rotting fruits flows
adrift in the chilling air around me.
Visions come and go; dreams rise and fall
back again into the subconscious.
Dreams, hopes and plans appear, then
vanish into the muddled memories
Of all the people whose lives I have been
fortunate enough in which to share,
Or sorrowfully enough in which to be a small part . . .
Some meaningful relationship, or some tragic
experience, some wasted point in time;
A compilation, a quagmire of sometimes
muddy, sometimes bright and clear
Hopes, dreams and experiences which I have
shared with some who were once,
For whatever reason, important in my existence, lie
here on paper . . . lie anchored in my heart.
A world of once young people: students; friends;
relations; sons; grandchildren and acquaintances.
Perhaps some were strangers who might (for a
fleeting, flashing or flagging moment)
Have affected my life in some way.
As my mind's eye fades along with my visions and memories,
People who, at some time or other, drift
into the veil of mist around me,
Like ghostly fantasies which seldom speak above
the faint, hollow echoes of years long past.

Sometimes, however, there is, for a moment,
a voice as clear as the church bell
Which a beloved one and I heard in melodic
tolling as we passed by on our way . . .
Sometimes there is only a whisper of murmured words . . . away,
Away in some far-off, distant land.
As I gaze into the misty reveries of life as I
have seen it, I search and wonder,
"Did anything really matter to anyone? Did the
experiences I think of really happen?
Were they all phantoms on the edge of my life . . .
On the periphery of my fevered mind?"
Perhaps they were my life. Perhaps they never were at all.
Far into the past, so very long ago . . .
Still, I have not forgotten the image though,
But the name was not for me to know.
Some father's son just sitting there
A mother's joy so young and fair
A mysterious form in the misty air
An image imprinted within my brain
That neither wind, nor snow, nor rain,
Although I try, but try in vain,
Can fade the sylph that yet remains.
Though the years have made my vision dim,
I stand at my window and remember him.
In summer, with vague expectation I walk among
Trees of apple, peach, pear and plum,
To see if he perhaps has come
Back home to me like the prodigal son.
The fruits are gathered, the leaves have blown,
And, except for memories, he has forever gone.
And so, through bare orchard, I walk alone.
But memories seem to ever stay
To haunt me . . . twilight, night, dawn and day.
Though I have plead them go away . . .
Yet, pray for the misty wind and rain

To the orchard bring him back again.
How strange not to remember when he first appeared.
I do not remember who he was, but I can sometimes recall a name.
Just a boy in an orchard someplace in time.
But does it really matter he ever came,
Since he never returned to sit beneath the red-apple tree?
When I first saw him there, on a summer afternoon,
His presence beckoned to me, and we stayed until the half-moon
Was high in the twilight sky.
The ripened fruits tasted sweet, as the juice
of joy dripped from our lips.
Apples, peaches, plums and pears . . .
I wonder if I shall ever see him there
When the warm summer breeze
No longer plays among the trees
And the cold, winter winds
Have blown and tossed the autumn leaves
Across the distant meadow.
Through the cold, misty haze
Of a morning in December,
At my window, I stand and gaze,
Then slowly I remember
How he vanished in the dewy air
If, indeed, he was ever truly there.
When the blossoms of springtime
Once again adorn the branches,
Perhaps I shall see him beneath
The white of apple, pear and plum,
Or among the pink of the peach tree blooms,
I will stand and gaze across the meadow
With the fond hope that he will come.
The complex tie of a shared joy
Leaves a memory so very dear
Of a young and fair orchard boy,
Who came from somewhere, far or near,
Then vanished into the twilight . . .

Leaving only a memory in the dark of night,
In the light of day, that haunts me through the years.
Perhaps it was simply an empty wish . . .
A narcissistic reflection in the mist.
The prettiest marbles I've ever seen . . .
Marbles of yellow and marbles of green,
And I remember red, and purple and blue . . .
And sometimes in the quiet of night, I remember him, too.
How could I not remember the first day that we met?
Some things, it seems we should never forget.
We were the best and dearest of friends
I do not remember what happened that caused it to end.
But even today, there is an emptiness still . . .
A space in my heart that nothing can fill.
He scattered my marbles all over the ground.
Sadly, I stood and watched them roll around,
Then I picked them up slowly, after he had gone.
The dust blew in my eyes as I watched him run on.
When he was gone from my view, I wiped at my dusty tears
. . . And I hid my marbles and my heart away for years and years.
We had played in the sand and we had played in the grass,
While the sweet days of summer flew by us so fast.
We ran like wild horses, and flew with false wings . . .
We sang and we danced and we did secret things.
Without words, we made vows that we really meant to keep,
But tomorrow and yesterday never can meet.
I sing and I dance and I play at life's games
And I have known many people, but remember few names.
Both fortune and sorrow have been mine by chance.
And love even gave me a fleeting glance.
I seldom look forward, nor backward to us,
But sometimes I see marbles rolling 'round in the dust.
What, except for death, can fade the sylvan form . . .
Sometimes still, sometimes a storm.
Sometimes I wish for the misty wind and rain . . .
I hope and I hope, but I hope in vain . . .

I hope and I wish him back again,
Or see him forever gone to from where he came,
And forever banished from my fevered brain.
I dream of joy, and find it sweet,
But lose it somewhere in my sleep,
For when I awake it is always gone,
And I find myself again alone.
When I was young and still could fly,
Sometimes angels would pass me by.
They never stopped to say, "Hello.".
They only peered at my life below.
Through many years, I've wondered why,
As life so swiftly passed me by,
They did not see me in my plight,
As I floundered along in my own flight.
Since I can no longer lift my wings . . .
No longer hear the wild goose sing . . .
Discontent and grounded I wait
For joy that should have been my fate.
But Wait!
Many times I held it in my hand,
I simply dropped it again and again.
The webs we weave should not be strong
Enough to silence the throat of life's joyous song,
Nor to weaken the voice of right and wrong.
Within the webs, among the thorns . . . there is a rose
That diminishes, that vanishes all cares and woes.
The pricks and sticks throughout the days
Were softened, faded by his gentle ways.
His loving eyes, his sunbeam-smile
So frequently my time beguiled . . .
More than a heart deserves to ask,
He gave a joy that ever lasts.
And, still, he clears away the webs life weaves,
And heals the scars that trouble leaves.
I will hope that he clings to youth, until a rose full-blown.

Laughing through darkest nights, until adulthood dawns.
Like roses, youth will fade away,
But its power and its fragrance stay:
That sometimes on a splendid day.
The radiance of sunset and moonbeams play
Above in heaven's fading blue,
Together in shades of brilliant hue,
They will bring joy to me in images of you.
Though heavy clouds may linger low,
Magnificent will be the evening glow,
If I may keep those images until I go.
I'm holding winter in the palm of my hand,
While you are searching for springtime in Everland.
I am grasping for snowflakes.
You are plucking a rose . . .
I am living in yesterday's reveries,
While you are making tomorrow's memories.
Our happiness can be found somewhere in between
The chill of winter, and the warmth of spring.
The shiver of age blows through my days,
While the bloom of youth reveals the truth
That God in Heaven knows I am grasping for snowflakes . . .
You are plucking a rose.
Winter holds me in the palm of its hand,
You bask in summer splendor in Everland.
Gold and brown, falling down . . .
Autumn leaves to the ground.
Lacy leaves lie, lingering low
Beneath the icy rain and snow,
Awaiting for warm winds of spring
And colors that sweet summer brings.
The soul of leaves from years long past
Hold memories that forever last.
So, it was only a fantasy, a ghost-ship of a dream
With sails so thin that they only wilted in the wind.
Nothing more than a fantasy.

Though bright as the beam of moonlight's glow
Reflecting on the dark below,
Only a fantasy floating in the oceans of my heart . . .
How could it fly and lift its sails up to the sky?
Was it really only a ghost of a dream . . .
A spark of light above the dark of dreary evening . . .
A dream worth remembering? No it was life!
With dimmed eyes, with time gone by,
Where rotting fruits in the orchard lie,
Through the misty nights . . . in sleepless dreams
I still can see him there, it seems . . .
And on sunny days, warm and still,
I look at my marbles on the window sill.

SLEEPING ON THE SURFACE

By
ROBERT BERTRAND

SLEEPING ON THE SURFACE

PROLOGUE

When daylight fades, but lingers long enough for the twilight to captivate my attention and embrace me in its peace and calm for a few treasured moments (as it can at only one other time during a twenty-four hour period; that being the few minutes just before daybreak when the candle-light sun is not yet in view upon the horizon), it is possible to experience perfect peace; that joy which never grows tiresome, as all other pleasures can. Sleeping on the surface has often compensated me with this opportunity. The dawn and the twilight hours are much the same in that both have the power to force into my being, the great pleasure of the peace they offer. Also, they are much the same as the quality and character of my sleep; simple moments lingering on the surface between here and there, now and then, sooner and later, higher and lower, ... awake and asleep. Being a morning-type person as well as an evening-type person can be a bothersome handicap. It is like trying to do split-shift sleeping. Morning types can sleep at night. Evening types can sleep as late in the mornings as their life styles will permit. Those few of us who possess the two types of sleeping patterns are both blessed and cursed. We can delight in both of God's daily gifts, the sunrise and the sunset. But when do we sleep? Perhaps never, as far as good, quality sleep goes. We doze somewhere on the surface during the night (unless we are also affected by a full moon, in which case we get an even lesser quality of sleep and fewer minutes), and hopefully can find a quiet place to catch a few winks during the day. Such is life.

It is a small country church. The cemetery has no more than thirty or forty tombstones, in remembrance of that number of people passed. But how many dreams lie buried with the remains of those bodies, those stilled hearts that once held so many grand and wonderful dreams; dreams that could have, had they been followed, brought so much joy, not only to themselves but to countless other loved ones, and even to others whom they had never met. Unfulfilled dreams lie buried in the Siloam Cemetery, because they were not understood by families and friends, perhaps dreams that were even considered absurd and ridiculous . . . . even dangerous! And so, many people have taken their dreams to their graves with them, in order not to upset, disappoint or shock relatives and friends. Here, beneath the green grass and violets of early spring, beneath the humidity of hot summer days, beneath the brown leaves of fall and the infrequent snows of winter, lie decayed bodies that once had beating hearts which at sometime in their lives were filled with untold dreams, unspoken words of stupidity and ignorance or words of great wisdom. No one would ever know the significance of those dreams that no longer exist, that are only memories of the stilled and decayed hearts that lie below the grass, as still and cold as the tombstones that shine ghostly in the light of full moons, year after year.

The dreams inside my own heart cry out so loudly that the moon hides behind a cloud for a moment before reappearing to shine brighter than it has ever shone before across those graves; so brightly that it clarifies my dreams, more brightly, more clearly than ever. As I leave the cemetery in the middle of the night, I know it will probably be the last time that I will ever see the tombstones marking the resting places of my parents, brothers (including the unfortunate miscarriage), as well as an assortment of uncles and aunts, grandparents, and several childhood friends . . . . The presence of death hovering here in this cemetery (perhaps even wavering, like butterflies over blossoms), cause me to wonder why I am still above terra firma.

This visit to the cemetery on such a moon-lit night was *before* I had decided what I would do with the rest of my life, but *after* I had decided that I would indeed do something with it which could be considered (at least by myself) worthwhile. The clear message I received from this visit among the dead, was that life is not over until God says it is finished. I determined (or it was determined for me) that I would not sit in front of a TV set, miserably pondering my future. God had started it where He wanted it to start, and now He could finish it whenever He chose. To me it did not matter where I would be in this world when my heart stopped beating, so long as it was not filled with regrets of unfulfilled dreams, and goals which God had set for me. Challenges, chances, and assignments, and ways and means would be presented to me in time. My greatest task, because of my impatient nature, would be awaiting through the nights and days, or perhaps even months for me to hear my heart speak, as I was accustomed to listening to my mind instead of my heart. However, I knew that He would implant His message in my heart in His own good time a time when He had made me ready to meet the purpose of my present existence. I knew that in my heart lay the answers to my future.

Zebra finches (I think that is what they were called). For several months I enjoyed their un-musical "chirping". Then on a bright spring morning, as I went to clean the bottom of their cage, and to add a new supply of seeds to their feeder, I found that one of the tiny feathered things lay stiff at the bottom of the cage. Due to my lack of knowledge of the species, I did not know if it was the male or the female. It made no difference; the obvious loneliness of the surviving mate left me with a sad heart for days thereafter. I was vaguely familiar with the poor fowl's loneliness. My empathy for the lone caged bird became increasingly more pressing with each passing day. And I began to resent its existence as a widower (or widow), because it reminded me constantly of my own status. Thoughts of releasing the bird, who by now was surely feeling imprisoned in the cage which in the past had been a happy home with a loving mate, were more and more becoming obsessions in me.

Before many days had passed, I was sure that the little creature wished to flee its imprisonment. So did I. And so, on a brilliant sunny morning in April (flowers and blossoming fruit trees embellished the surrounding gardens, and wild honeysuckle and dogwood painted the evergreen wooded areas with white, pink and yellow), I gently embraced the tiny bird within my palms, took it to the edge of the rose garden, lifted one palm and watched my little friend fly swiftly over the meadow and into the deep green of the forest never looking back as a gesture of "thank you" or "good-bye". I knew that its chance of survival was **nil**. My consolation in my having released it, was in knowing that for a day or so (or even a few minutes), I had given it freedom I had given it freedom to use its God-given wings. Using those wings for the purpose for which wings are given was justifiable reward.

That was before I set myself free in order find my own reward of peace and serenity (perhaps even a day of extreme happiness) far away from my cage of invisible bars. And although they were bars which I could not see, still I knew they were there, blocking my every thought with iron-like power, a stoppage which I had not the strength to break through and escape to freedom, as my little bird had been allowed to do. I looked between, around, over and under the impasses before I realized that freedom was someplace I had yet to see, to find. I had yet to identify it. That was before I actually faced the reality of the fact that I was already free; that the door to my cage was open. My lack of freedom had not been a cage of surrounding problems and misfortunes, but simply of not understanding that somewhere among them was an open door through which I could flee as swiftly as my little bird and flown. Sometimes one had to arrive at the open door in order to discover that one has actually been imprisoned in the first place. This comprehension was what set me free. The next day I left my cage, carrying nothing but the clothes on my back and my hopes and dreams. I didn't look back.

Greentown was no different than any other Southern, back-woodsy little town as far as I could see; but then I never looked very closely at it. Like all small towns, there was a Church Street. If every street in town which had a church located on it was named because the church was on that street, then every street in town would have the same name. There was a College Street, but in the years of my living in that fair city, there was no college anywhere nearby. There was a college on the "by-pass", but on College Street. Main Street, Elm Street, Oak Street, Walnut; every little closed-depot town has them. And when it comes to the denizens of Greentown, well, the good Lord did the best he could with what He had to work with.

On Pine street is where I met Pearlene. We were neighbors. I seldom had given her a second look. I have always heard that if you meet a red-headed woman, you had better make sure her hair is dyed red, and not natural. You can't trust the temperament of a true redhead. She can twist your mind with the power of an Alabama tornado. Pearlene did not have red hair. I did. She should have seen trouble from the start, since my hair is (or was in my earlier days) as red as blazes. I was a cute child, everybody said so. I was a good-looking teen-ager, everybody told me so. I was a handsome young man, everybody agreed. As a man, I was hot. I still had no freckles in those days. Fair skin, green eyes, red hair (in which everyone wanted to play, run their fingers though) and a charming, if somewhat freaky, personality, seemed to attract a lot of people. When I was not smiling, evidently my expression was like a cross before a vampire, as people avoided starting conversation with me, avoided even making eye contact with me. I did not realize that I had a temper that put people off. Pearlene helped me with that after we married. When I would become angry, I would simply go off by myself someplace and rant and rave my rage away. Although she herself liked my hot temper, she said that it could get me in lots of trouble if I did not learn to control it. In spite of my temper, my red hair, the non-awareness of my flirty ways (or perhaps because of them) Pearlene, for whatever reason, found me attractive enough to marry me. By the time we married, she knew from experience (as was commonly known by a large percentage of the town's population, by both men and women) that I had the biggest penis in Greentown.

Pearlene stayed with me long enough to have two kids for me; a girl and a boy. Neither of them took my red hair. Pearlene was a good woman. I could depend on her. But that was before the murder. She didn't leave me because she thought I was guilty (she was unsure about that), but because of all the publicity, gossip, family interferences and such. She just couldn't take the pressure any longer, so she took the kids and went to Birmingham where she landed another teaching position immediately. Pearlene was not a pretty woman, she had sun-dried skin, a slightly hooked nose, and frizzy, chicken-shit brown hair, so like many other Southern women that are **unlike** the cute Southern-belle types with their little turned-up noses, well-kept, unfried hair, and sweet little Minnie Mouse voices.

I was glad that Pearlene left, because at that particular time many unkind things were being said about me, and I did not want my kids hearing all the crap that the crappy people of Greentown were saying. Also, I did not know that it was going to be a permanent arrangement (that Pearlene and the kids would not come back). I missed the kids, but I did not miss her.

After the investigation was over, I was sure that there were those people who were not convinced that the young woman had cut her own throat, and that there was not really a murder committed in my basement. There was no evidence that I had killed her. I had no reason, and was not arrested due to lack of motive, or evidence. I left Greentown, too. There were too many people, even former friends, who did not believe the girl had committed suicide in our basement, where she had posed for me many times. If she was in love with me and wanted me to leave my wife to be with her, it was not my fault. I would never have left Pearlene for any woman, but I would never go to live with her again. Her uncertainty about my guilt (she knew my temper) and the nature of our married life was not conducive to a reunion. With my share of the money from the sale of our house, I went to Paris, France to continue painting and to study the masterpieces in the museums.

The young Frenchman entered my studio and, looking at my red hair, said in a nervous voice, "Je m'appelle Jean-Pierre." He had seen the sign I had taped on the outside of my studio (which served as my home as well), and had knocked on the door to inquire about the modeling job.

I said, "Take your clothes off." He did, and I hired him. I said, "You can call me 'Red', 'Carrot Top', 'Copperhead', or you can call me 'Alex'. That's my real name. Alexander Cox."

Weeks earlier, Jean-Pierre had been happy that he had passed the "audition" the first time he had posed for Alex. He was very self-confident with what he had to show. His ability to pose as a model was what had caused his nervousness. He had not been concerned whether his anatomy would please the artist, and he had practically flaunted himself in front of Alex, who was interested only in how lights and shadows would fall on the model's body. Jean-Pierre was not very tall, nor stout, but he had tight, firm muscles and a very flat belly; a young swimmers body. Alex would have preferred to have hired a somewhat older man, with a bit of flab and some wrinkles of character which can come only from a lifetime of interesting living. But he was intrigued with Jean-Pierre's excitement over the possibility of posing for him. Also, the young Frenchman was the only person who had knocked at his studio door in response to his sign, "Male Model Needed".

Over a period of several weeks, Alex was able to do sketches of many different poses with which he was very pleased. The learning process pleased him more than the results produced. Jean-Pierre was happy to earn extra money to pay for his school expenses. He was regretful when he was no longer needed, and that he was only a vehicle for Alex to better himself as an artist. He had actually hoped that a painting of himself might hang in a gallery, or at least in a shop window.

The flight from Paris to Cairo, Egypt would have been a perfect time to sleep, even with the lay-over and flight changes. But sleep was only for those who could deep-sleep. Surface sleeping on a flight was little more than an image, a shadow of sleep: dreams in such shallow sleeping were no more than day dreams. Marcella had pushed her long, straight hair to one side, over her shoulder where it fell next to Alex's face. It smelled good. She fell into a deep sleep. She looked so peaceful, so innocent that I ("I" am sometimes "Alex" . . . explained later) wanted to cry, not for her, nor for me, but for Pearlene. I don't remember how Pearlene looked when she slept. Maybe relaxed and peaceful, or tired and wearisome. I don't even remember seeing her asleep. I remember that her hair was not alive with the heat of life. Marcella's hair probably would not have looked a lot different from anyone else's hair from a distance. I remembered the first time I ran my fingers through the shiny strands, and when I buried my face into its lush, fine, velvety (or was it silky . . . the feeling.) excitement of her hair that fell across her pillow, the ecstasy overwhelmed me and I cried. Hers was not brown, nor was it a color for which I had ever heard a name. It was that beautiful mouse color that only a few women possess. Those who have it, know that they have it, and they let it grow long because its quality is rare and it is their crowning glory . . . for some, their only claim to beauty.

I was never quite sure from where in Southern Europe Marcella had come. She called no place home, as she traveled the world, stopping briefly where she found someone she wanted in her life for a period of time. Presently, I was that someone, the joy of her life. I first met her at Le Pont Alexandre III in Paris, just before I decided I no longer needed Jean-Pierre. The scene of this bridge was very picturesque (having been painted thousands of times by master artists as well as unknown painters such as myself. I had painted among the real artists of Paris, hung out in little "artist colonies" trying to learn and steal art tips, and had been made fun of and laughed at by some of the best. I was not intimidated in the least. I didn't give a fat rat's ass what remarks were made, even by the few friends I had made. So, I had come to the bridge here above the Seine River to paint. My mediocre painting suddenly became a beautiful portrait, as Marcella stepped from behind my canvas. It was as though she were a woman in a famous portrait who had stepped right out of a frame and into my life. My friends had all said my paintings were ugly, pure "merde", they said. And we would all have a good friendly laugh. Now, when they saw me with Marcella, nude in my studio, they had only remarks of envy. She had commissioned me to paint a portrait of herself. During the next two years, as we shared life together, I painted many nudes of her, none of which were good. She did not care if they were bad, She bought all of my paintings for several thousand dollars. She took one snap-shot of her favorite painting with a small camera, and we left Paris. All of my paintings were left behind in her apartment. The landlord was instructed, quietly, to do with them as he pleased. Marcella did not want to be bothered with packing and shipping. And the fact was that she had no place to ship them. I hated leaving them behind, but after all, they were no longer mine, and I was happy to have more money than I had had since Pearlene and I sold our house in Greentown.

Our luxurious room in the Nefertiti Tower of the Sheraton Cairo Hotel had a balcony above the Nile River. In the cooler part of the evenings, we sat there and enjoyed the wine and great food and each other. After several days of visiting pyramids, sphinxes, and dozens of tombs and religious architecture, we were exhausted of the endless columns standing in the sweltering heat; temperatures reached degrees far higher than any heat I had ever experienced in the South, in Alabama. Marcella booked passages for us to cruise the Nile River for a few days. She had also booked reservations at the Conrad Hurghada Resort on a beach of the Red Sea. The cruise on the Nile was a great experience for me, but Marcella was soon bored with the nightly entertainment. She was becoming bored with me, I thought. One night we were entertained by a small band of very black (Nubian) young men. As the band entered the show room with their instruments, one young man looked at my red hair and smiled, revealing the whitest teeth I had ever seen, and dimples in his cheeks to get lost in, visually speaking. This flirtation had not gone unnoticed by Marcella. The Egyptian music was nice, and I was happy when it was over. I wanted to get some sleep, or at least some rest if sleep did not come. As I was descending the staircase, I turned to see that Marcella had stayed behind in the crowd and was speaking with the young black man. I waited for her at the foot of the stairs where I found a comfortable chair. We went directly to our cabin. I asked, "Were you complimenting him on his singing?"

"No, I invited him to visit us here." She answered, casually as she was disrobing to get into the shower.

"When? I thought they were only on board for tonight." Alex stated.

"Money will get you anything, even an extra night of entertainment from the young man you so hungrily smiled at." Marcella said.

"What do you mean? You paid him to stay on the boat, and to visit with us?"

"No, I paid him to stay on the boat and sleep with us." She answered.

"Are you out of your mind? Marcella, you can't be serious . . ." The knock at the door stopped him from finishing his sentence. He said, "I'll get rid of him. He still has time to get off the boat with his group." Alex opened the door to see the deep dimples grow even deeper as he smiled, showing his pearly whites again. "Come on in. Entre vous. Enter!"

"Pull him in, Alex. He doesn't know what you're saying. And you won't understand a word he says either. No one but a Nubian can speak Nubian."

Alex gently pulled the beautiful, black boy inside. He began to undress immediately.

Marcella had her reasons for hiring the young black beauty's company. Alex would soon learn of her reasons. At that time, Alex was only thinking of what a beautiful painting he could make here and now, had there been paint, canvas and brushes available. The night was long for him, and sleep did not go below the surface of the pelting waves of consciousness, in which he painted many brush strokes of black.

The bus ride from the small town to the Red Sea resort seemed to last about five or six hours. Again, Marcella slept. I stayed awake. Maybe I floated somewhere on the surface of sleep, for I now became "I" again, instead of Alex. So now I will try to explain how sometimes I speak of Alex as though he is another person and not myself. As I try to sleep somewhere in vague unconsciousness, or when I am awake, but dreaming as though I were asleep, I see myself in many settings, with many different people, in many different circumstances, and in many points in time. I see myself from a distance in time and place, and I spy, or re-live, or dream of Alex's experiences. Reality brings me back into myself. And so it is then that I am I again.

The Resort hotel was beautiful. The food was great; foods I had never tasted, nor seen before were in abundance. I especially liked the fresh fruits and melons that were harvested along the banks of the Nile River. The beautiful clear blue water of the Red Sea was the most inviting I have ever seen, and I have seen many beaches in different countries. Breezes kept us cool. Also, clothing was optional. I chose not to wear any, after looking around at other guys. I knew I would be an object of envy, and of interest for the other sun bathers on the white sand where the inlet of the sea allowed gentle waves to sweep upon the shore. Most of the men were nude. Some were not, perhaps due to modesty, or perhaps due to the possibility that they were little. Who cared? It was a time to be different, shed ones worries, inhibitions and clothes. I expressed my opinion to a few. Some rejoiced in the freedom they felt after my persuasions, in spite of the fact that they had less to show. Marcella and I entertained in our room; both women and men, old and young, from many countries including a few Asians who could not resist staring at my glistening red hair. From lying in the sun so much, my freckles were becoming more interesting to on-lookers than I would have liked. However, I learned to like my freckles after I became used to them in my earlier years; that happened after I was told by a special someone that my freckles added to my sex appeal. I was never sure if Pearlene found them attractive, but I remembered a young woman in my basement telling me how lovely my freckles were. I think that Marcella was sincere in her compliments of them. I had doubts, however, when I walked back from the beach to our room to find her in bed with a slightly tanned, blue-eyed blond German guy. He did not speak English. However his body language was loud and clear.

At dinner that night, I asked, "Does this mean we part here; at the Red Sea?"

"Appropriate enough, I guess." She answered. "I have made your flight reservation. You leave tomorrow. Early. You need to get to sleep early tonight. I've had a porter move my things into the German's room." She said.

"Do you even know his name?" I asked.

"Why would you want to know that?" She asked.

"Am I allowed to ask what is my destination?" I asked.

"New York City. You have money to last for awhile. I have kept you from your art work too long. I'll call a friend who will meet you at JFK. He will help you to get serious about your painting. He'll make arrangements for your living quarters. I regret having to cut your vacation short, but it is time for us both to move on. I have already. You will when you get to New York and become involved in painting again. You're good."

Get serious. Forget what the Paris artists said about your paintings. Remember only their suggestions that will help you to improve, and forget the rest. Just don't lose your own style. My friend can be of great help to you." Marcella smiled, as she got up to leave our table. "Now, if you'll excuse me, my desert is waiting for me." She walked away. Her "Good-bye" was a slight wave over her shoulder without looking back. I never saw her again. My bus ride to the nearest airport city was pleasant. I was surprised that I did not miss Marcella at all.

"Alex! Over here!" The voice came through the noises of the crowded airport. The man came up to me, smiling amiably, and took one of my bags.

"I thought you would be holding a sign with my name on it. How did you know that I'm the guy you were waiting for?" Alex asked.

"I figured there would be only one badly sunburned, freckled face, redhead on this flight! Turns out I was right." The rather handsome, older man said. Alex guessed him to be in his late fifties. His thick hair was iron gray, nice wrinkles gave character to his good facial features, and his bright blue eyes were especially attractive, with little crow's-feet wrinkles about the edges. He held his well-exercised body erect, which probably made him appear to be younger than his real age.

"Are these your only bags?"

"Yes, Marcella insisted on our traveling light."

"She always did. Collecting too much stuff, she said, caused you to carry too much baggage. Of course, she was not talking only about material things. She was referring to emotional and mental baggage, mainly. She never really needed a lot of fashionable clothes, nor accessories. She's still a perfect beauty in any kind of garment, wouldn't you say?"

"Yes," Alex agreed. "Where did she get all of her money?"

"By the way, I'm Jeff Jenkins. I doubt if she gave you much information about me. In her twenties, she was a photographer. Majored in it in college. After she collected her . . . . shall we say 'inheritance', she has majored in men. She has been generous with her money, when she meets a poor guy she likes. And she's added to her fortune through well-planned marriages. You were her latest 'major' subject." Jeff said.

"Still, she never considered marriage to me." Alex said.

"Like I said, her marriages were well planned. You had no money." Jeff said.

"Well, she has now dropped me as her major subject. Some handsome German guy is her main study now." Alex said, and he was able to laugh about it.

"She photographed models. She could have been one herself, such a beauty as she was, with a model's fine figure."

Jeff said, "She was a model, briefly, for me. She posed for many paintings for me."

"In the nude, of course." Jeff suggested.

"Yes." Alex could not laugh now, because of the wonderful, lovely pictures that came to him mentally.

"She figured that if she ever needed to work again, which is doubtful, that she could always go back to photography, but old models cannot go back to being young again. That's why she was a models' photographer instead of a photographer's model." Jeff led Alex to a taxi. "But enough about her. Lets concentrate on you." He said.

"What would you like to know?" Alex asked.

"After my long telephone conversation with Marcella, your life is an open book. At least I have the major contents page. She related all she knew about you to me. But you should know some things about me, so that you can feel a bit more at ease, since I'm sensing that you are a little uncomfortable in New York City in the hands of a perfect stranger . . . well, at least a stranger, as I am far from perfect. However, I hope you can overlook my flaws."

"I am a failed, would-have-been artist I have many contacts; art gallery people. Important wealthy people who support the arts as well. And I have no family. I live alone in my very expensive apartment. When I say my apartment, I mean I own it. I was a greater artist at using my good looks in my young days, than I was at painting. I've done well financially and made many wealthy friends; hence my having done well financially."

"How can I fit into this slightly abstract, though attractive, picture of your life?" Alex asked.

"I like my coffee at nine a.m., black and very hot. It will be convenient for you to bring it to me, in bed, because you will be living with me, and because the maid sets the coffee pot timer to have the coffee ready by nine. That's your only obligation to me.

"Marcella thinks that you have real potential, real talent. She wants me to push you hard toward developing that talent. Just because she's through with you, relationship-wise, does not mean she does not believe in your abilities. If you are worried about finances, don't.", Jeff said.

"You pay for nothing except your paint and canvases, and she told me you have a bit of money left from selling paintings in Paris." Alex had to laugh, as she was he only one who had bought his paintings, all of her, and all of which she did not want. He knew that she had wanted only him, and only until someone else attracted her interest.

Jeff said, "You don't even have to stay and have your coffee with me, if you choose otherwise, as I am used to having mine alone."

"And if I choose not to have mine alone, may I stay?" Alex was curious. "Most certainly. As long as you like."

When Alex moved in with Jeff, he had no idea that he would still be living with him five years later. Alex was at his bedside every morning at nine with hot coffee. Occasionally, he would stay for awhile.

During these years, Jeff had arranged several shows for Alex's paintings. Then he caught enough attention that reviews were being written about his work. There were mix opinions by the art critics. Alex listened to public opinions at his shows; he found that the ones who like his art, had only a mild liking for it. Those who did not like it, hated it. Once in awhile, some good-hearted bejeweled old lady would purchase one, paying far more than it was worth, in her efforts to buy him along with the painting. Jeff knew them well, and he was quick to have them back off.

Alex could hardly believe that Jeff was seventy-five when he died suddenly of a massive heart attack. He still looked young, and had the energy of a much younger man. Jeff's death was not taken lightly by Alex. It was not because of his love for Jeff, but because it made him start to thinking about his own age, his life . . . his death. He was approaching forty. He was alone. He had not seen his children in almost ten years. He wanted to see them.

Annette met Alex at the Birmingham Municipal Airport. He was stunned at how beautiful his daughter had become. She drove him to a restaurant. "I thought we would be going home . . . . I mean, well, you know, to your house." Alex said, surprised that they were going to a restaurant in the middle of the afternoon. "I was hoping that we could all eat together tonight."

"Dad, that's not an option. Neither Daniel, nor mother agreed to see you. They tried to get me not to meet with you. You need to realize that Daniel hardly remembers you, and mother remembers you too well." Annette said.

"Was I really that bad? Our marriage, our family life? How do you remember it, Annette?" They sat at a nearby table, having helped themselves at the salad bar. Annette ordered coffee.

"We all remember that you left us and we've grown up and moved on without you in our lives." She said, with a bitter tone in her shaking voice.

On first seeing him at the airport, she had run to him, held tightly in their embrace, but at once had begun to grow distant and cold.

"Does Daniel really believe that I left. Has he not been reminded that it was your mother who left and took you with her? Never mind. It was for the best at the time." Alex said.

"I don't know what mother thinks or knows about you and that model who died in our house. She chooses to never speak of it. Yes, it was best for us to leave. And even if you had come to us, I think that mother would have divorced you anyway." Annette shared her opinions without hesitation, and her voice was no longer shaky.

"Why, then, does Daniel dislike *me* so? I never asked for a divorce, and I never did anything to cause her to want one." Alex believed what he was saying.

Before his death, Jeff had begun to refurbish his apartment. He was bored with the collection of antique furnishings. Living among these old pieces of furniture and items he had brought from countries in which he had traveled, he explained to Alex, was making him feel old. He wanted to have around him new and modern things which would make him feel more youthful. Alex agreed that he should make changes that would give more light and color to the apartment. Work on the remodeling of the apartment had already begun when Jeff died. It was now Alex who had to follow through with the project. The contractors and construction men already had instructions as to the refinishing of the apartment itself, but Alex had to sell off the antique pieces and select new furniture. Jeff had taken care of legal documents to be sure that Alex would own the apartment after his death. Also, he had left his now quite small amount of money in a joint account, so that Alex would have easy access to it whenever he needed it. It took most of the money in the account to pay for the refurbishing of the apartment. The money Alex got from the antiques was more than enough to pay for the new furniture. He had consulted an expert in feng shui in order to achieve balance and calm in his life among color, shape, space and image. (It was through this same feng shui expert that he was to meet Shirley several months later).

After the apartment was completely redone, Alex still had his own money which would last for awhile, but he realized that it would be gone within a year unless he should begin to sell more paintings. He would probably need to get a job. But he had no training. His sleepless nights, in his new bed, became worrisome nights. What was he to do? At his age, with no training in any trade, no experience with any job and without friends in high places who cared enough for him to hire him out of loyalty to friendship, left him up shit creek without a paddle. The more he thought about it, the sadder his circumstances became.

Jeff should never have begun the make-over of the apartment. What was he thinking?; spending so much money when there would be so little left on which to buy food and other necessities. Alex for the first time in his life, found himself in a situation in which he had to think of how he would survive. Presently, he was selling more and more of his mediocre (a generous adjective for his work) paintings to wealthy, lonely widows, and a few old men who were not alone, just lonely. Money can buy one happiness, if only in a very brief time frame. For a few years, he was able to survive in this way. But, as he was now termed "middle-age", there were fewer old ladies who wanted his work. He was not young anymore, and many of his older friends were no longer on the top side of the turf. His red hair, which many found to be sexy, was fading away to a dull gray. Since it had been necessary to cancel his gym membership, he was gaining weight around the middle, and was losing the stud-like strut in his walk.

On the celebration of his birthday (mid fifties), he found himself alone with a bottle of wine, cheese and brown Russian bread; his birthday dinner. The feng shui designed apartment did nothing for his low-down feeling. He would never think of killing himself, but there were times when he thought it would be good to die, providing the dying would be painless. After all, it seemed that the better part of his life, which at this time did not seem to be so great, was over. As he was pouring himself a second glass of wine, there was a knock at his door. He opened to the gentle knock. A handsome young man stood in front of him. Had it not been for the small picture in his wallet (the one Annette had given him), he would not have recognized Daniel, his own son.

There were semi-pleasant greetings. Alex invited Daniel to sit on the couch. He chose a chair farthest from where his father sat on the couch.

"Are you here to wish me a happy birthday?" Alex asked, with some amount of sarcasm, feeling rather certain that he was not there for that purpose.

"No. I didn't even know that it is your birthday. I don't even know how old you are. How could I?" Daniel still had not smiled even a tiny bit.

"If you had asked, you could have known."

"Mother did not like it when I asked anything about you. Besides, I didn't care."

"You could have asked me. I sent birthday cards, Christmas cards, too, sometimes." Alex said.

"I never saw any."

"So, you think I didn't care about you, and you didn't care about me. Then why are you here?" Alex asked.

"I never said I didn't care about you. I said I didn't care how old you are. What mattered to me was that I had no father. It still matters that I have no father." Daniel said, accusingly.

"If you will let me, I can still be become your father, Daniel. I can try anyway.

I don't know how. I didn't grow with it as you were growing up, and I suspect that parents usually start out knowing very little about it. By the time you're grown, we become experts at it. So, due to past circumstances, I'm no expert, but I can try to be a father of some sort. You can teach me what is required, and I know I can learn how to be your father, unless you think it is too late. I know for sure that I can give you some good advice concerning living. I've made the mistakes that help you to learn what not to do." Alex said.

"Mother has taken care of that. I've had all the advice I can stand."

"Then what, may I ask." Alex was asking, as he poured them both another glass, "is it that you want from me?"

"Money." Daniel answered, quickly, but in a matter-of-fact manner. "Money is all I want from you. At least for now, that's all

I want. After I get to know who you are, maybe I'll want more. It depends on whether you're someone I like."

"Be cautious. You might even learn to love me." Alex warned.

"I already know how to do that, Dad. I just don't know yet if I *like* you." Daniel showed a warm smile. Alex wiped the tears from his eyes, not even trying to hide them from his son.

During the next three weeks, the father learned much about the son. The son learned less about the father, but enough to know that he was a man he wanted in his life.

Father and son prepared for themselves a delicious dinner for the night before Daniel was to leave to go back to the university. They had enjoyed their time together, going to the theatres, dining out and seeing all the usual sites that tourists come to see in New York City; places which Alex had never been during his years of living there. He had never cared to go to see the Statue of Liberty. He had seen the smaller one in Paris, and had enjoyed the experience with Marcella. He had no interest in the view from the Empire State Building. He had seen all the art museums and galleries, but it was much more fun than ever before. He had to think why. He felt that he must be really stupid, really growing old, or that he had missed out on the best part of life, when it occurred to him finally, that the fun came from sharing these experiences with his son.

"Daniel, sometime, when you see your mother again, I wish you would let her know . . . . somehow, in your own words, that I'm ever so proud of her, I mean for the great job she did in raising Annette and you."

"So, you think we turned out OK?" Daniel smiled at his father's confessed approval.

"There is no way I can ever tell you how much it means to me that you are here. I always knew I could love, but I didn't know how hard, how deeply . . . how real . . . ."

"OK, Dad, I get it!" Daniel's soft smile was there again. It was a smile that Alex was seeing more and more as the days passed.

"I just want to be sure that you know. Now we need to talk about your reason for coming to me in the first place; money." Alex said.

"To be honest, I've already gotten what I really came for. I got my dad back. But, yes, I do need money. Mother has put me through the first two years of college. I'll be a Junior next term. But she does not have the money for me to continue my studies. And I have a long way to go. I'm studying to become a lawyer." Alex beamed with pride over his son's ambition. "I realize that even though you seem to live well . . ." He paused to look around the fantastically "feng shui-ed" apartment. "I realize that maybe you don't have extra money, and that's OK. I can borrow."

"What? You think I'm a starving artist, living in the lap of luxury. Just because you don't like my art, doesn't mean others don't."

"Well, Dad, to be perfectly truthful, keeping in mind that I'm no art critic, I think your art is, well, *crap!* I cannot imagine that you are actually selling this stuff." Daniel laughed as he looked at one of his father's paintings, the only one of his own in the apartment."

"I think we can manage to get you through law school without your owing a fortune in student loans after you finish." Alex's assurance was very convincing, and Daniel was greatly appreciative and relieved.

"My son, the lawyer! My daughter, a school teacher like her mother." Yes, Alex thought, Pearlene had done it right.

The next day, Alex went to the airport to see his son off. He was returning to The University of Alabama at Birmingham. "You have my address. Let me know where to send you the check, or what bank to have the money transferred to. And find yourself a good apartment. You need to be comfortable while you study."

"Dad, my place in Southside is sufficient. I won't waste your money on luxuries."

Alex hugged his son, and told him, "I didn't know how much I love you. Thanks, Daniel."

"I always knew how much I love you, Dad, even before I knew you . . . before I knew how much I *like* you."

The next day, Alex found a real estate agent. The apartment sold quickly, and for no small amount of money. Most of the money went to Daniel. For himself, he kept only enough to rent a room and to live on while he was trying to figure out what he would do with the rest of his life.

Alex sat on a faded, velvet-cushioned bench, one of three which were spaced in the center of the gallery to which Jeff's will had given him entitlement. Fewer artists were using the gallery now. He knew that he would soon have no artists wanting to use his gallery if he did not make some renovations. Repainting the walls in fresh, neutral tones was a great need, as the old paint was peeling and dingy. Lighting should be improved, carpets and benches should be replaced. These improvements would cost a large amount of money; money which he did not have. As he sat looking at the bare walls, trampled carpets and faded benches, he thought the situation hopeless. He could possibly sell the gallery, but he really wanted to keep it. One day soon, Trane would show his paintings here. Unless improvements were made quickly, it would be useless to show the young man's paintings; important people (meaning people with more money than brains) would not come in, even for the champagne.

An acquaintance of Alex (one in whose company he had been at many of Jeff's parties) advised Alex to join him for brunch. He would arrange for him to meet Bennie Drake-Hardeman.

"Who the hell is Bennie Drake-Hardeman?" Alex asked.

"Only one of the wealthiest connoisseurs of the arts in New York City. I'm sure you have met Bennie at some time in the past." Albert, the friend, said. "I think that Bennie will foot the bill for the renovation on your gallery if you will be willing to show some amount of appreciation. No strings attached, otherwise."

On the morning of their scheduled meeting, Alex and Albert arrived before the third party.

"I understand about the 'appreciation' which I am expected to do! How old is this Bennie. What does he look like?" Alex asked, without the slightest bit of interest.

"Only a bit older than yourself. And as for looks, see for yourself. Here she comes now."

"A woman? Bennie is an old woman?"

"As far as I know, yes. Had you rather do an old man? Be nice!" Albert advised. Bennie was laden with bling bling, far too much for an early brunch. Alex was sure not to show disapproval, since the meeting was laden with significance. She was attractively "put together", evidently having been up for hours. The meeting went well. The following weeks of showing "appreciation" were bearable for Alex, and so pleasing to Bennie that she not only paid for the improvements for the gallery, but even arranged for and supervised the work. Alex's aging might have diminished his looks, but not his size. The gallery was most attractively re-done, and word was soon out that it was a place to exhibit the finest works of young artists. Alex was soon relieved of his expectations of gratitude to Bennie, for she had met a young artist whose career she would promote (with properly shown appreciation, of course).

Trane was still in high school. Alex found it necessary to spend less time with the young man, and so he left Albert in charge or arranging for the exhibition of his paintings. When Alex had first met him, it was his talent that got attention. But now it was becoming obvious to others that Alex was showering too much attention on Trane the artist, instead of the young man's art work. It was a good idea for Alex to go away for awhile, in order to get Trane off his mind, as well as to not be a diversion to Trane's concentration on his art studies.

Alex convinced himself (or lied to himself) that he simply had 'itchy feet' again. He would take a walk a long walk. Better still, he would take a run! Even better, he would go far away from where he was. Going away could cure a vacancy blight that he never even knew he had. That somewhat ever-so-slight feeling of discomfort, or that overwhelming desire to learn what else there is in the world beyond what was in his present life, was reason enough to leave New York again. Many times he had had the thought that the place, the life, the world in which he had spent the previous year, might not be the one which was best for him at that point in time. Maybe it was not even the most enjoyable place. Just because God had dropped him off at a certain spot in the universe did not mean that He meant for him to remain there for long. Perhaps for some people . . . . , people with dear friends, a familiar life-style and even a loving family . . . . in other words, a comfort zone, would be the best place to be. But he had none of this. Perhaps God had other things in mind for him, other purposes which Alex should check out. He was definitely considering change. Who knows what awaits 'over yonder, out there, in a different place'. Maybe joys of which he had never even dreamed, perhaps someone who desperately needed him, or an environment in which he could be more creative in ways he never thought possible, using talents and gifts he did not know he possessed, were awaiting him patiently. He became more impatient with every glimpse of Trane. He would take a hike.

Often, Alex had talked long hours away in his small apartment with Trane. He talked to the young man of "youth power"; refuse to litter our language with four-letter words, just as you refuse to litter our roadsides with beer cans, or cheeseburger wrappers. The surest way to eliminate such crime (and it is a crime, not just a shame) is abstinence. The money spent at coffee houses (not named here) could possibly bring a certain amount of joy to someone who would appreciate a new book. Young and old alike could have difficulty purchasing some good reading due to lack of funds. Alex found himself making an impression on the young man in his company. He found also that he was making changes for the betterment of his own character by dropping some of his own bad habits. "You are powerful, Trane." He had said. "You are hope, you are destiny! Do not take your responsibility and your study of art lightly. Do not underestimate your strength, your wisdom, your ability to make changes for the better in the lives of others as well as your own through your paintings. Your life is not your own to live in a day-to-day routine of self-indulging activities. Indulge your passions in directions which will give the most people the most benefits. You may then realize your own benefits from being placed on God's green earth. After all, your life is His . . . . He gave it to you just as he will take it back when He is ready.

The more often Alex spoke to Trane, philosophizing and giving what he thought to be guidance, the more he realized that he was simply preaching to himself, and then he would realize that even though it might be too late for himself, perhaps it was good advice for such a capable young man. Surely Pearlene had given his own children such advice, for they had turned out well. But Trane was not his son. It was time for him to distance himself from the young artist. Alex chose to go to China.

I was lying in the grass when I first met Mai Ling. Springtime had arrived. The Chinese Government had ordered the heat in buildings to be turned off weeks earlier. It was still cold inside my apartment. While sketching a picture of budding plants along a pond's edge, I found the grass in the park to be quite warm from the welcome sunshine. That was where I first saw her. I, lying there like frost over the unborn grass . . . . she, passing by like a warm breeze of summer. She had stopped to look at the flowerless water lilies when she noticed that I had taken up my sketch pad and pencil to draw her. She smiled and accommodated me for a few minutes before turning away to disappear beyond the rocks yielding a bubbly little waterfall. The trickling water sang along with my heart. The young woman was too beautiful to become my model, her body too perfectly shaped, the halo over her shiny black hair to heavenly to allow her to become an image on paper. She would never be a model for my drawings, but she would be the object of all that was important to me in my experiences in Beijing, China. The fact of her youth compared with the years of my age in no way interfered with my organized plan to know her, and to know her well. "Alex", I told myself, ". . . she is too young, and you are too old."

I did not listen to my mind. My heart was speaking the truth in a loud voice. Many a flower can bloom between May and December. Life is for the living (while death is for the dying), and I was suddenly living the life of a twenty-year old who was begging to come out of the body of a selfish old fool who had just fallen in love. Her young life and my older life shall meet somewhere in time, and intertwine as the rose and the briar on the graves of Sweet Willie and Barbra Allen. We shall find our happiness somewhere between the chill of winter and the warmth of spring. In some distant tomorrow, she will rejoice in memories of our time together, while my joy will lie in the present and the hours of our cherished past; dreams somewhere in our brief times of yesterday. While the chill of age blows through my days, the thrill of youth will brighten her ways through years yet to come. While I may hold winter in the palm of my hand, she will be searching for springtime in forever, ever-land on a hillside plucking violets. And I shall be in the valley where the snowflakes fall upon my brow. The bloom of roses will still sweeten her cheeks, as the frost of age runs through my veins. The sun of her days will bring the dawning of new beginnings, while for me the dusk of evenings will bring the night bird's song of days gone by of fading memories and anticipated endings. But during our time together, yes, many a flower can bloom. The flower of her smile of May will melt the snow of December from my heart. I shall walk slowly through the winds of winter, hand in hand with her as she waltzes through the summer breezes. Many a raindrop can fall, many a teardrop can fall, many a heartache can call, but many a cherished pleasure can become a treasure to remember in the cold, dreary nights and the long weary days of December. Alex did not believe in regrets, and I knew when I met Mai Ling, that regardless of how long or how short would be our time together, neither of us would ever look back with regrets. From the first glimpse of her, she made my cold heart to sing, and breathed warm life into long forgotten dreams which I thought to be buried in the passing of years gone by.

"Why do you do this, Mai Ling?"

"What? What is it that I do which is in question?" Her large oval eyes always had the look of pleasant surprise, but when confronted with such an ambiguous question, the look was more of a startled response. And at such a time, I would always gleefully anticipate her answer, because her moods, although constant in their gentility, were as that of a capricious breeze, always surprising me, always thrilling me. Mai Ling was quite beautiful, with her black eyes that appeared to exude their own sparkle, rather than to reflect light from other sources. Her flawless light skin was so radiantly clear and smooth that strangers found it difficult not to touch her face or her hands and arms, as though she were a section of fine silk in a market place. The long straight hair, which shown of sunlight, moonlight or candlelight (and even from the whiteness of our pillows) would fall in untangled, smooth strands far down her back, when I would release the combs from her velvety mane. For me, it was the most powerfully sexual feature about her physical being. It was her propitious nature which had first appealed to me. I observed her almost to a point of reconnoitered observation for several days before I was sure that she was genuine in her behavior toward the customers who she served in the restaurant, in her meeting with friends on the street, or even with strangers with whom she would talk while waiting for a bus or the subway train. Finally, I was urged by an uncertain feeling, though strong, of some desire (and of ennui) to know her.

"You have to explain your question. I do not know what answer you wish of me." She said.

"Why do you make me fall in love with you more and more each day I am with you? Why do you allow an old man to adore you more abundantly with each night we spend together?" I asked. Her answer was in her eyes and her smile. Before she could speak, I said, "Don't. Don't say anything. I am sufficiently pleased with the answer you just gave me.'

Mai Ling was most beautiful when she was in her traditional dress of red and gold. The collar was high on her lovely, thin neck, reaching up to her perfectly shaped, round chin. A narrow band of gold braid enhanced the collar around her neck and down the open slit revealing her graceful throat and a bit of titillating cleavage. The floor-length dress, with the same gold braiding around the bottom, allowed the toes of her black pumps to show the gliding motion as she moved across the floor with the grace of Michelle Kwan's world—renowned spirals on ice. Mai Ling would take only a few seconds to pull into a tight bun atop her head, the black hair that was as shiny as the black leather pumps on her tiny feet. As a receptionist in an elegant restaurant, she was required to wear the traditional outfit. A jade bracelet of an unusual color was her only accessory.

Dressed to go to her place of work, was when I thought her to be most beautiful. I often thought that most American men dreamed of Asian women looking just so. When it was time for sex, one of my greater pleasures in all my life was letting down her long, silky hair, before letting her down onto my bed.

She moved in with me, because my apartment was more comfortable, with Western style toilet, larger refrigerator and balcony views of the city (and, of course, because we loved each other). During the evenings when she was not at work, a favorite place for us to enjoy the evenings with our wine and her deliciously prepared meals was on our balcony. I had been to her place of abode only once. She shared the shabby little apartment with a relative, perhaps a cousin, whom I had met only that one time. He was friendly, but distant. Mai Ling explained that he was seldom in the apartment, as he worked as a guard and usually slept in the building in which he worked. On seeing her apartment, it was not easy to imagine such a beautiful, clean, intelligent young woman living in such squalor. She showed no embarrassment, nor shame, but the enthusiasm with which she packed her few belongings into a plastic bag, showed me how pleased she was to leave the apartment and move in with me.

During the many years of my life, I had loved many times. Each time, my loves had seemed different, and better than the ones before. I knew, as I was approaching my seventy-first birthday, that this love truly was different, and that it would be my last love.

But the experience I had in Beijing is not about Mai Ling and me. This part of my life is about a love longer lasting than ours. In an apartment in the building where I was staying, while I visited the great sights of that city, sketching the many scenes of interest, I met an older couple. I would often see them as I was sketching in parks where there were little rock gardens, softly flowing waterfalls, ponds colored with water lilies (green, pink and white, blissfully lying upon the surface of the water), ancient little bridges, and people who might have been ancient; it was sometimes difficult to detect whether one was aged or youthful. Sometimes I would see youth in the smooth face of a boy or girl, but in the eyes there would appear to be the fading glimmer of age, or perhaps the loss of hope which had once burned bright in those same eyes.

The couple (perhaps married, perhaps not), were very friendly people; people of interest to me. It was through my observation of them that caused me to realize the gift of my ability to love Mai Ling in a manner extreme and foreign to me. Their attention to each other, the looks they gave each other and the way the old couple walked so closely, so slowly (an important and revealing factor toward my own knowledge of special love) hand-in-hand around the courtyard and through the beautifully landscaped little garden areas around the high-rise complex of apartments, reflected my own feelings that I wanted to share with Mai Ling. I knew of her love for me before I knew how much I loved her. Although she had given herself to me completely, reciprocity on my part might never have happened, had it not been for the obvious which I saw in the relationship of the old couple, something I had never seen before. With great determination, I was sure to make the effort to do the same with Mai Ling with great thrill and wonderful enthusiasm which I had never experienced.

The old couple and I became casual friends (perhaps even great friends at moments). He was Caucasian (from America) and she was Chinese-American. They were considerable older than myself, perhaps approaching their late eighties. I learned that they had met in Beijing while he was on a business trip to China more than fifty years earlier, when few Americans were visiting China. They had married, (perhaps) and this was their first trip back. She had come to see Beijing once more. After almost fifty years, she was both thrilled by the fantastic changes of old to new and modern, and saddened by memories of what used to be, now gone, a vague image in the minds and hearts of some, completely forgotten by others, and never known, nor seen by younger Asian eyes.

On many of their strolls, I was invited to join them. Once, I sketched them as they sat on a stone bench, surrounded by roses and other flowers of every color and hue. Running about the courtyard were young children, whose mothers sat together, watching them play as they ran into and out of the mist from the spouting water fountain. I gave the sketch to the old couple before they left to return to America. As we said goodbye at the time of their departure, I knew that her tears were for her farewell to her beloved China. His tears, I was certain, were for her . . . . for whatever it was that she was feeling. My tears were for the gratitude I felt for what they had shown me of love.

In the days and nights to come, I would hold Mai Ling more closely, cling to her more tightly, appreciate her more sincerely; love her more deeply. On the night that she did not return home, I waited for two hours for the sound of the key in the door lock. Finally, I went out along the route which I knew that she took to and from work. The restaurant was closed. Back in the apartment, I waited for her to come to me. Then came the dawn of the day of my panic. I asked at the restaurant and was told that she had not come to work the evening before. I went to her old apartment. No one was there. I went to the few friends of hers that I had met, but none of them had seen her. For three days, I waited for her, knowing in my heart that she would not forsake me, hurt me beyond any pain I had ever felt before. The police in the area could tell me nothing. I was never sure if I even communicated successfully my concern, even after showing them her picture.

I left China the day after I learned that Mai Ling had been killed instantly when she stepped from behind a bus and was hit by a bicycle which had in turn caused her to fall under a passing car. The relative I had met once, came to my apartment to claim her personal belongings, and was able to relate to me in his broken English what had happened. I placed her few possessions in a box, keeping only one picture of her. The relative handed to me the jade bracelet she wore. He could speak very little English, but we both knew the sorrow we each felt.

Trane had never been out of New York City. His serious study of art had kept him sheltered from certain life-styles that had actually been a handicap to his painting. One must live life in order to tell about it in painting, dancing, writing, singing and acting. I had tried to live. I had been trying to help Trane to have new experience since the time I had met him after returning from China. I invited him to go to Greentown with me. I thought that if there is an opposite to New York City, it was probably Greentown. Also, I thought that it would be good that Trane should have his first community-expansion

experience (geographically speaking), in that small town in Alabama.
From there, he could go sideways or upwards, depending on the
effects of the experience.

My art show in Greentown was to open within a week. It would
probably close before the paintings were all removed from the
packing. I didn't care. We flew into Birmingham, rented a car and
drove on to the small town. On the flight, I welcomed Trane into
membership of the mile-high club.

News of my minor successes as a painter in New York, Paris,
Cairo, Beijing and other places to where I had drifted, had reached
Greentown, and my minor successes were big news in the small
town. Although I was barely "making it" as an artist, I would never
let them know. In spite of my exaggerated success, I knew that my
invitation to show my work in my hometown was not of interest
to the denizens of Greentown (I did not paint deer antlers, dead
turkeys, nor fat asses in tight, short skirts). I knew that they were
only curious to see, after all these years had passed, what Alex was
like. I wanted to see what I would be like back in Greentown. I
wondered if Alex would still be a mystery; a subject of gossip, a
man whose innocence some still questioned (concerning the young
woman who died in my basement), a man that would still be asked
to satisfy unfulfilled women whose husbands were now on Viagara,
levitra, cialis and various contraptions and stimulants. Only a tinge
of redish color remains in my thinning, graying hair. That would be
a disappointment to some. But I would not disappoint the poor souls
as far as my art work was concerned. I would have a professional
showing, fifteen or twenty of my best nude drawings and paintings
which I had retrieved and saved through the years. I was certain
that I was far more interested in seeing the reactions (and reading
the reviews) to my paintings, than Greentown was of seeing my
work. Some of the women with frizzy hair and outdated heels would
hide their excitement, after having viewed, with pretentious shock,
my nude drawings, until they returned home to their couch-potato,
beer-drinking husbands, at which time they would trouble them for
at least a bit of effort toward a long-overdue sex.

My paintings had arrived before I did. I was to unpack them and supervise the hanging of the exhibit, which would be in the old train depot, it having been recently renovated to serve the local artists as a gallery.

On the evening of our arrival at the hotel, both Trane and I were tired, hungry and sleepy. We took care of these needs after I decided that I would not call the Arts Council Chairperson to inform her that we had arrived. Since we had done the "mile-high" thing on the flight down South, we now wanted only sleep. My surface sleep that night fluctuated between "he" (Alex) and "I". Sometimes "he" could see me laughing at the sight of Southern Baptist women fainting in front of my frontal-nudes of men, right onto the gallery floor. "I" could see Alex and Trane being chased out of town in our rental car; men, women, and children throwing perfectly good tomatoes and fresh eggs at them. Sleeping on the surface can have its compensations, its fun times. I laughed away most of the night as I slept in wonderful consciousness, with visions of red, ripe tomatoes flying pass my head.

The exhibit was a success, for a few. There were actually a few genuine would-be artists who appreciated the show. There were a few closet queers who enjoyed it immensely even if they did not know squat about art. On the other hand there were teachers and parents who were herding their charges out of the depot so quickly that they might have been using cattle prods. Many came out of curiosity, others out of duty; the Arts Council members, the newspaper writer, members of the local art club and others who had not the slightest interest in an art show, but who suddenly felt it their civic duty to show up at the exhibit, even if they neglected to sign the attendance register. After the third day, no one showed up, and so I was told by the Mayor that it would be wise to pack up and leave town before the local ministers became too upset. At that point, only one had suffered heart failure after having viewed the show. One wonders what it was about the show that brought on his excitement. When Trane visited the preacher at the hospital, he made a solemn promise, at the minister's own invitation, to come back to visit him as soon as he recovered from his attack. We did not see the weekly newspaper before leaving town. If there was a critique, we were spared from it.

The trip to Alabama was a great experience for Trane. It had turned out to be very educational, artistically speaking, also. He had taken pictures of some of the most beautiful scenery in America. "Who knew that Alabama was such a beautiful state?" He had been mesmerized by its stunning greenery, its flowers, its hills and dells, even the farmer's fields of growing crops. "I knew there were stars in the sky, but I never knew there were so many. And the sky is actually blue!" For months to come, Trane would paint pictures of Alabama sunrises and sunsets, old barns and fences and some of people of whom he had taken snapshots. Weeks later, I noticed one of the pictures was of the sister of the girl found dead in my basement. She had come to see my show.

I thought about what Trane had stated, "Who knew that Alabama is so beautiful?" I knew the answer. The people who live there. They prefer not to spread the word too far abroad in order keep people like us away.

Alex had never been quite certain of many things in his life. If he had lived in "days of old", he would have been the last person on Earth to become convinced that it was not flat. One thing he knew for sure was that love does exist (he had acquaintances who would argue the point), because he had loved. A few people had even loved him, which he felt was a remarkable factor. More remarkable was the fact that I *knew* they had loved me, despite my being Alex. Trane was one of those people.

"I have located a small house in the country, Trane." Alex announced one evening as the two were having an inexpensive dinner in a small cafe. "I'll be leaving New York within a few weeks."

"Why? How is it that I know nothing about this plan?" Trane was surprised and hurt.

"I knew that you would try to stop me, and I cannot stand up against you. So, I settled all the plans before telling you." Alex explained.

"No, I wouldn't have! I would not have tried to stop you. I'll go with you!" Trane was adamant.

"It's in the mountains of the Western part of North Carolina. And *no!*, you may not go with me."

Even more hurt, Trane said, "I don't know why . . . . *Why?* Why can't I go with you? I'll get a job. I'll pay for my . . . ."

"Trane, stop! Please don't argue with me about this. I have made plans for you plans that do not include me." Alex said, with tears swelling around his eyelids.

"No, I'm going with you. The mountains will be a great place to paint beautiful pictures, and I can help with expenses! I have worked before, when I was in high school"

"Listen to me, Trane. If you go with me, you would always enjoy painting, for sure, but you need to continue to study. With me, hidden away in the mountains of North Carolina, only you and I could enjoy your work. But if you continue to study the masterpieces in Europe, someday the whole world will know the joy of your works. You can be that good!"

"But, Alex, I can't go anywhere! I have no money. The paintings I have sold in your gallery have barely brought in enough money to pay for paints and canvasses. You know that. You have given me a place to live, fed me, bought my clothes . . . ."

"I have sold the gallery. You'll have enough money to last a few years, providing you live like a starving artist in Paris. And I have enough left over to see me through my remaining days." Alex said.

"Alex, you are so good to me. You're such a wonderful person to do this for me. But there is this other problem which you can't fix if I go to Paris. I'll miss you too terribly to ever be happy there." Trane was sincere, and certain that it was true.

"You don't have to be happy to become a great artist." Alex responded. "When you get to Paris, you will soon forget about our good times, and then you will be making more good times than you ever dreamed possible. If you ever grow tired of the good times in Europe, you can come and find me in the mountains."

Clicking teeth, old-man grunts, the odor of age if they had become part of me, I had not noticed. I did not realize when I had actually, truly grown old. However, dropping off to sleep while watching a favorite TV show, and even in the warmth of the early spring sunshine in the parking lot at the local Wal-Mart, had definitely become an actuality which I rather enjoyed, a luxury, really. Sleeping on the surface of gentle waves of wakefulness . . . . *no wait*, that was not new. I had always, at least as far back as I could remember, lain in my bed floating somewhere between some point in existence between awake and asleep. In some slight degree of sleep, I was always aware of anything happening around me at any given moment; the tick-tock of clocks, the gentle wind whistling around outside the corner of my bedroom, the rustle of green or brown leaves near my window, the barking of some distant, lonely dog . . . the flushing of a toilet in the next apartment. If there were times when I slipped from the surface into a deep, dark pit of sleep, for no apparent cause I would awaken with a start, smothering for air, wishing for deep breaths of cool, refreshing air. How amazing is air, wind! What life it gives to us, oxygen for the very blood that is pumped through our tiny capillaries that join our arteries and veins. Often, I have been awakened by the lack of the precious air, the result of which would throw me into a panic, arousing me from my bed as quickly as I could throw back the bed covers. A rush to the West window, where there could be seen lights from the elevations (the moon, the stars, the distant hazy lights above the envied, sleeping city) would ease my "take-flight" instinct. Often I would already have on my running shoes before the relief of life-saving air would ease my panic. During days of dread or anxiety, I would need to remind myself to breathe. Gradually, my pounding heart would slow to a normal, steady rhythm, bringing with it delightful peace which would shroud my body, bathing me in perfect harmony to my existence with the sweetness of night. After such experiences, I would often remain awake for the rest of the night, involving myself in creative activity at my drawing board. I knew (or felt) that if I returned to my bed, I would drift from wakefulness down to the surface of the ocean of sleep, and there I would float throughout the night like a piece of driftwood over the gentle waves above the darkness of the sea depths. Sleeping on the surface. Was it a gift or a curse? I feared sometimes, that if I sank into the depths of a deep sleep, I would never again find my way back to the surface in order to rise to the state of awake.

It is amazing how, for some, the experiences of past life can slip from one event to another. The memory being able to skip over certain unpleasant, even tragic events, but able to keep some that are worth remembering in the body of consciousness, is an important gift. And without intention, being able to drop others so deeply into unknown parts of the brain that they can sadly or wisely be left silent: Alex was thinking, "Where have I been? Let it lie still and quiet. That which is important will surface, even if while I sleep."

Alex remembered the day he said goodbye to Trane at the airport. He remembered when a few days later he had left New York for the last time. He had not reflected on the past as he drove through the mountains and valleys to his new home. He had tried to think only about what life would be like from that time on. He had tried to envision some kind of future, but his mind's eye was blank, and his heart was empty. Afterward, there had been no regrets.

DECORATION DAY AT ANTIOC EAST

BY
ROBERT BERTRAND

DECORATION DAY AT ANTIOC EAST

THE NARATOR

Character: The Preacher is the narrator.
              He is an older man.

(Preacher Mason is placing a bunch of wild flowers on his wife's grave. He turns to talk directly to the audience) I was just placing flowers on my wife's grave. She's been dead she died a long time ago. But I still bring flowers. It's "decoration day" at Antioc East Church. Every Spring, the congregation comes to spend the day at the church. We give the church a good cleaning, and we clear the cemetery of faded silk and plastic flowers and shredded ribbons and bows. And we cut back the growth of early briars, black berry vines and running wild roses before they get out of control and cover the entire cemetery. Weeds are cleared away from the fences and from around the tombstones. Some people bring baskets of food . . . . fried chicken, fried pies, cakes, potato salad, tea and sweet lemonade. These are spread out on the long wooden tables under the shade of the large old oak trees around the church yard. I do not bring anything. I am the preacher, and I just come to preach and eat, and to enjoy the fellowship and singing. I've already delivered an inspirational message, we had prayer, and now everyone has finished eating, so it is time for some singing. Before we leave, the entire cemetery will be decorated with bright, new . . . . though mostly artificial . . . flowers . . . . they last longer. A few people just come to bring flowers, they don't come to sing and pray, (in the church, backstage, we hear singing.) Well, the singing has started, so I'll go back inside the church.

YOU'RE A GOOD GIRL, MISSY

Characters: Mary Sue, a teen-ager
                 Grandfather, older man

MARY SUE

(she is a teen-ager with long straight hair. Her dress is cotton with flower print. Her lips and cheeks are too red and her heels are too high. She walks, clumsily, to the grave and places flowers carefully on the grave.) I miss you, Grandfather. I wish you were here to fuss me out when I stay out too late and when I wear too much make-up. Aunt Helen is good to me, but she has her own life. She has very little time for me she don't want to be bothered with me. We don't talk like you and me used to do. I don't have anyone to tell me what's right and what's wrong. Don't misunderstand, I KNOW right from wrong. You taught me that much. It's just that I need to hear you say, "Now, Missy, you know better than to do that!" I want to be good . . . to do what's right. I'm really trying to be good. But sometimes I get so lonesome and blue, well, I just can't help myself. I just don't have the will power to tell Johnny "no" when he

GRANDFATHER

(He appears from behind tombstone.) I never meant to make you feel like a bad girl. You're a good girl, Mary Sue. You've had some hard knocks in life. Losing your dear mama and daddy like that. Having to leave all your friends to come live with and old prune like me. And then I pulled this one on you. (regards the cemetery with a gesture) So you had to move again and leave your new friends to go live in HELL with HELEN. In the last three years, you've been in three different schools. You've lost the three people who loved you most. You've lost all of your old friends. All except that JOHNNY boy.

MARY SUE

He brought me here today, Grandfather. I thought it would be a good way to get him in the Church, but he wouldn't go in. He's just sitting in the car waiting for me.

GRANDFATHER

Be careful of that boy, Missy! He could get you into a lot of trouble.

MARY SUE

I know. But, like I said, I'm trying to be a better person. And I'm hoping that I can help Johnny, too.

GRANDFATHER

Just don't forget the things I tried to teach you. I wasn't ready to die. I didn't want to leave you so young and helpless and vulnerable, and nobody to see after you but your Aunt Helen. She ain't fit to look after no young lady like you, Missy.

MARY SUE

It's OK. I'm doing fine. And I know that all those bad things that happened to me is no excuse for failing in school and for doing some of them things I've been doing. So, I just wanted you to know, I'm TRYING to do better, (she looks nervously toward offstage car) Well, Johnny's waiting in the car, so I'll go now. (she walks away while Grandfather is saying his last lines)

GRANDFATHER

"You're growing up, Missy. When you don't blame hardships for bad behavior, it means you've got your mind straight . . . . for growing up. (she is off stage right) Comeback any time you want to and don't let no fool boy fool you.

BRING ME VIOLETS

Characters: Adam, an older man
Brian, a man in his thirties
Young Man, maybe 20

Brian, thirty-something with a younger friend, walks over to Adam's tombstone. The younger man pats Brian's shoulder and slowly walks around through the cemetery and offstage right. Adam, an older man, appears behind his tombstone.

ADAM

Is he the one?

BRIAN

(Holding flowers) What One?

ADAM

THE one!

BRIAN

I told you a thousand times that you are "the one". And I emphasize ONE, because, as I said so many times, I believe there is only one true love for everyone.

ADAM

Not true! It's just a matter of opening up yourself spiritually, mentally, emotionally and, of course, physically.

BRIAN

Well, so far, I haven't gotten beyond "physically".

ADAM

So, you have fucked him! Was it good?

BRIAN

(casually) Like a covey of doves fluttered out of my ass.

ADAM

That's what you always said when we did it, so I guess it was as good as it was with me? . . . . that's a question.

BRIAN

As sex goes, yes, he is good. But you and I never had sex without love, and, as you know, sex does not compare with making love . . . . which is always what WE did . . . . except, perhaps, for the first time we did it . . . . on the hood of my eighty-seven, red Subaru . . . . on a dark country road, under a billion bright stars.

ADAM

At least a billion!

BRIAN

That was the only time we just had sex. After that, we always made love.

ADAM

(looking at the flowers Brian is holding) You brought me flowers. Thanks for remembering.

BRIAN

I remember everything, Adam, (he places the flowers on the grave) All day long and most of the nights that's what I do, think of you.

ADAM

That's why I want you to find a new lover, like that young man waiting for you over there. He's cute, well-dressed . . . . and I know how important that is to you . . . . he's good in bed, you say, and what else? Not a hairdresser, nor a florist, I hope . . . . and please tell me he's not a ballet dancer.

BRIAN

He does have an artistic flair. However, he is pursuing a career in teaching advanced math at the college level.

ADAM

So, he's good-looking, well-dressed, intelligent, and a good fuck! He sounds perfect for you.

BRIAN

Adam, I still love you. I still miss you. I still cry for you. I cannot help it I don't want anyone else.

ADAM

But you can't have me. I cannot come back to you. You have to start to live again to love again.

BRIAN

I don't want to love again. I had rather live with my memories of our life together, than to start over again. I'll be alright. I prefer it like this. So don't worry about me.

ADAM

Actually, we don't worry here. But dying doesn't mean that we stop loving and caring for you those of you who have not come over yet. I care for your happiness . . . happiness as you know it THERE.

BRIAN

Really? I'm glad you still can care for me and be concerned about me. Because sometimes . . . . sometimes in the middle of my lonely nights, I feel you near me . . . . not just at night, but during the day when I have to face the daily problems, I feel your love. Just like when you were still here, I can feel you lying beside me. Sometimes . . . . Adam, actually, sometimes I still make love to you. Did you know that sometimes I still get off with you? Just like we used to do it . . . . only you're not really there when it's over, not there to hold and . . . . and just be there.

ADAM

Sure, I know about it. We don't go blind when we cross over here!

BRIAN

Well, then, don't you miss it too? Do you miss it as much as I miss you?

ADAM

No. We don't miss anything here. We have everything we need and want here . . . . and I would never want to come back.

BRIAN

(he is beginning to whimper . . . a few tears) But I can't stand it. Sometimes I want you back so badly, that if you can't come back, then I want to come to you. I want to be with you.

ADAM

Whoa! Wait just a fucking minute! Get that kind of thinking out of your head, Baby. You have years of life ahead of you, and they can be good years or bad years. It's entirely up to you to determine what kind of life you will have. Life is for those who still have it, to live anyway they choose. You still have it, so make it precious and make it good. You can exist in a world of happiness, even when there is sorrow around you.

BRIAN

Please don't lecture to me. I hear enough of that from my family and friends even from him. (he indicates the young man who has drifted onto the stage again) I remember all the things you told me while we were waiting for the time when you would grow old and leave me. At the time, we didn't know that you would leave so suddenly the way you did. But you had time to give me plenty of advise and instructions about how to have a life after you.

ADAM

Then you remember that I told you that my greatest wish for you, was that you would find some young man who would make you as happy as you made me.

BRIAN

But what you don't seem to understand is that I'm not completely unhappy. I'm more content to live with our past than with a future involving someone else.

ADAM

But, Sweet Meat, that is not living. It's dying a slow and insignificant death. If you have a life, then LIVE it! But if you are choosing death, then make it count for something.

BRIAN

Don't even go there! You know how I feel about what you did! It was a foolish risk you took. So what if you saved a life . . . . you gave up your own, and in so doing, you took away everything meaningful in my own life, too.

ADAM

I'm sorry I suppose. I'm not sure that we can actually feel regret here. We do look back, however, at least I do. And I know that I still love you. And, therefore, I wish that you would move on. Don't misunderstand. I appreciate your loyalty to US, to your and my relationship, I mean. I appreciate your visits to my resting place, the flowers you bring and the tree you planted which, by the way, has to go.

BRIAN

What do you mean it has to go? Why? (He touches a small tree nearby)

ADAM

Rules. They say nothing larger than a rose bush. It's a rule. You know, death has its rules, too. There are more rules in life, but at least you can choose to follow them or break them. In death you have no choices but to follow the rules. You just keep quiet and do what the rules tell you to do.

BRIAN

That must have been a rude awakening for you, since you always chose to break all of life's rules.

ADAM

All except one. I never broke the rule that says be loyal to the one you love.

BRIAN

But now, you're telling me that I should.

ADAM

I'm not there anymore. When I left, our relationship left also. There's nothing left of it. You are free to start all over again.

BRIAN

Easy for you to think so, but I'm the one left with all the memories . . . . memories that will never set me free . . . at least, not free enough to ever have what I had with you.

ADAM

But free enough to have SOMETHING. So have it, whatever it turns out to be. (the young man is now moving closer to Brian, still gazing at epitaphs on other graves) Maybe something with him.

BRIAN

He is nice. Very nice. But don't you remember the difficulties, the trying times, the hurts that you and I went through before we began to feel comfortable with the fact that we might have a successful monogamous relationship? Remember those first months of doubts and mistrust we went through? I don't think I could go through that again.

ADAM

Yes, I remember. And I remember, also, after we had been together several months, those first weeks of sheer unmitigated ecstasy, no, RAPTURE . . . when we realized that we had everything we wanted in each other and that we trusted, not only each other, but ourselves, to never betray our love. When I knew I could trust you, it was great. When I was sure that I could trust myself, it was the greatest. Then, after a few years, we realized that we had a history together, and that made it even more special, because we could say, "remember when?" . . . . and we could laugh and cry together.

BRIAN

There are no short cuts to making that history. Time together is the only way to have it. And that history is still with me. But now, I have to laugh and cry alone and that's no fun!

ADAM

Of course it's no fun! That's why I'm saying make another life for yourself . . . . with him. You said he's a nice guy . . . . and he sure has a cute ass! Take him home and fuck him!

BRIAN

You still have that sense of humor, (smiling)

ADAM

And one more thing. Stop coming out here. This place is for the dead, not for the living.

BRIAN

You really don't want me to come back?

ADAM

Maybe once a year . . . . on decoration day. You know how I like violets.

BRIAN

OK. Maybe I'll see you then, (he turns to the young friend) I'm ready yeah, I'm ready, (he looks back, but Adam is no longer there. The young friend puts his arm around Brian's shoulder, as they walk away. Brian looks back once more) There really were a billion stars that night, wasn't there?

ADAM

(still out of view)At least a billion!

A MATTER OF TOUCHING

Characters: Calvin, late forties.
                 Donna, his wife, early forties.
                 Ellie, same age as Donna

Calvin is late forties. Donna is early forties. He is waiting for her, standing behind his tombstone.

CALVIN
What, no flowers?

DONNA
(she enters stage left while he is talking) You don't deserve flowers.

CALVIN
First, I get a cheap funeral, lousy tombstone, then I get no visits for weeks. And, now, when you finally come, I get no flowers.

DONNA
I didn't come to bring you flowers. I came to tell you that I am finally free of you.

CALVIN
I don't understand (no emotion). Explain.

DONNA

I intend to. Although, even after I do explain, you will never know the hurt, humiliation, embarrassment, headaches and yes, heartache, . . . you caused me.

CALVIN

What? Because I died? I couldn't help it, you know. My time came . . . so I split. I had a one-way ticket on the midnight train, so to speak. I had no choice but to use it.

DONNA

But you left only after you ran up a hospital bill and doctor bills totaling over a hundred and fifty thousand dollars.

CALVIN

It's not like I did it on purpose.

DONNA

You didn't even try to improve. You didn't even seem to WANT to get well. You just lay there and died.

CALVIN

It's true that I wanted to die. Who wouldn't? Broken arms, ribs, legs burnt to a crisp. Remember how handsome I was? A real ladies man, everybody said. Not after the crash, though. The fire ruined my face. There wasn't much left of me . . . not even a brain. I had to call it quits. I couldn't live like that. What kind of life could I have had in that condition?

DONNA

And what kind of a life was I left with? Do you ever think about that? Sometimes I just wanted to die myself. I couldn't make my car payments. I had to sell the house to pay part of your hospital bills. I had to take a job at the grocery store in order to pay rent on the hellish little efficiency apartment I had to take. Katy had to drop out of school, (pause) Has she been here?

CALVIN

No. (no emotion)

DONNA

I thought she might have come before she left.

CALVIN

Before she left? Where did she go?

DONNA

To California. When she dropped college, she couldn't find a good job, so she married that Adams boy with the rings . . . you know, the ring in his nose . . . . and ears, and tongue . . . . and God knows where else. Anyway, they went to San Francisco.

CALVIN

Aw shit! (first emotion) I hated that bastard. Why did you let her do that?

DONNA

Don't blame me! You're the one who drove while drinking and died and left us. I was not in control of her. I was not in control of myself. I was not in control of anything! Everything just went spinning round and round, and down the toilet! I lost my car, my house, my dignity my friends. I had nothing left. I'm forty-one years old and I have NOTHING . . . . nothing to even prove that I ever lived.

CALVIN

Don't you have memories? That's what you're supposed to say when you lose a loved one. At least you have your memories. And you're forty-three. I lost my life, not my memory.

DONNA

What memories? The lies? The cheating? The hypocrisy? What fucking good are memories like that? I'm trying to forget!

CALVIN

I don't know what you're talking about. I thought we had some good times. What about when we first married and we lived in New Orleans?

DONNA

(easing up a bit)Yeah. I do remember those years. The Mardi Gras the quarter. Yeah . . . and Atlanta, too. I remember that little garage apartment. It was even smaller than the one I'm forced to survive in now. But we were happy then. And then we moved here and bought the house . . . . and Katy had the swing set in the fenced—in back yard and (coming out of her reverie) but all that was cancelled out when I went through your things, as I was moving out of the house.

CALVIN

What happened then.

DONNA

Like you don't know, you son-of-a-bitch!

CALVIN

Hey, be kind to the dead!

DONNA

You don't deserve any amount of kindness.

CALVIN

So you discovered my . . . what I did?

DONNA

Damn right I found out! Receipts for gifts you bought for HER. Things you bought for her and charged them on our credit card things that I have to pay for, now that you are gone! Love notes from her. Little books of matches from the motels where you took her. I checked it all out. And I never stayed in a motel in my life. Why not me, Calvin. Why didn't you just take me to a motel it would have been fun, and paying off the credit cards now might not seem so awful.

CALVIN

You checked it out? Did you meet her? (no emotion)

DONNA

No, I didn't want to. Well, maybe I did want to see what she was like. But I was afraid of what I might see.

CALVIN

What do you mean?

DONNA

Well, I guess she was younger and prettier than me. And I just couldn't take any more.

CALVIN

Well, you guessed wrong. She's about your same age, and she's not prettier than you.

DONNA

Then, WHY? Why did you have to have an affair with someone with no more to offer than I had?

CALVIN

I didn't say that she had no more to offer than you. There are other things besides beauty and youth.

DONNA

You mean you had an affair for money?

CALVIN

No. It wasn't that.

DONNA

Oh, stop it! Why then? (she's crying now) Why her? Why did you choose to be with her instead of with me? at home where you should have been.

CALVIN

(he is thoughtful, earnest) Because she touched me, Donna. She touched me.

DONNA

You mean physically?

CALVIN

Yes, she touched me physically, as well as other ways.

DONNA

I touched you physically, too. I tried to make you happy. I tried to satisfy you . . . in every way. You cannot say that I didn't!

CALVIN

That's just it, Donna! You tried to satisfy ME. You tried to make ME happy. I never knew if YOU were happy. I never knew if I satisfied YOU. She didn't try to satisfy me, she made herself happy just being with me. She touched me to satisfy herself. She wanted me, she needed me, she found fulfillment in touching me and brought me more happiness than I ever had with you. You did it because you seemed to think that it was your duty to make me happy. It wasn't.

DONNA

And now, on top of everything else, I find out that I was married to a crazy man!

CALVIN

I don't expect you to understand. You couldn't if you tried.

                              DONNA
Goodbye, Calvin.

                              CALVIN
Goodbye, Donna.

(Donna walks to stage left and stops at Adam's grave. She speaks to his tombstone.) Why did you have to pull him out of that car? If he had died in the wreck, the fire, at least I would still have my house and my car. (as she is exiting stage left, Ellie passes her to Calvin's grave)

                              ELLEE
I just came to say 'Goodbye' one last time, Calvin. I know that you don't care for flowers, but I wanted to bring them, so here, (she places a bunch of yellow flowers on his grave). I've met someone else. Life is too short to live without love. I won't forget you, but I'm moving on. (she starts to leave). Oh, by the way, why weren't you buried beside you wife? If you loved her so much and considering how much you told me you missed her after her death, I should think she would be here beside you. (shrugs "Oh well") and leaves.

LITTLE NAME FOR A BIG GIRL

Characters: Tina is thirty-ish
                 Robert is younger man who was with Brian in "Bring Me Violets"

She's thirty-ish. She's overweight. She walks from stage left and goes directly to grave with purpose, places flowers on grave. After five seconds, she sits on bench facing audience. After five more seconds, he appears behind her from tombstone. He does not speak. She knows he is there. He is the same handsome young man who was with Brian.

TINA
You know what they're saying? Everybody's talking about it. They're saying it was deliberate. Some guy even said, 'if I had to be married to that fat girl, I'd kill myself, too. (pause) I have three questions.

ROBERT
I might not be able to give you the answers you seek.

TINA
(she turns to look at him.) Come and sit with me. (he hesitates. She goes to him, takes his arm and they sit) Question number one: Was it deliberate? Question number two: If it was, why?

ROBERT

In response to your questions, I'll repeat what I said to you many times . . . . 'I loved you.'

TINA

Do you still?

ROBERT

Well, sure. Here, we love everybody. It's no different loving you than loving everyone else.

TINA

That really doesn't answer any questions for me.

ROBERT

I said that it is a response to your questions, not an answer. We cannot answer questions for you from here we don't even know the answers, Tina.

TINA

I always loved the way that you said my name. No one else ever said it with such gentle and . . . peaceful expression. Everyone else always called my name in a harsh tone, as though they thought that a fat girl like me did not deserve such a dainty little name as "Tina". Sometimes, I would think, 'You can't be talking to me, not in that tone! I am pretty little Tina' . . . . and then, of course, when I realized that my parents called my name in the same tone of voice that everyone else used, well, I became a very concerned teen-ager.

ROBERT

I KNOW. You told me all about it. I tried to get you to put it all behind you. To forget it. Just let it stay in the past where it belongs.

TINA

It's not in the past anymore. It's all come back since you left.

ROBERT

The way a person calls your name is no measure of their love for you.

TINA

Maybe not, but it's a clue. It sprinkles ones mind with seeds of doubt. They say, 'Tina' (with great resentment in her voice) like like I don't deserve to be a Tina . . . . like I should be an Ethel or a Mabel or maybe a Bertha.

ROBERT

If you had been given one of those names, you would have been the same person I loved so much. So what's the difference?

TINA

My parents just couldn't believe that I was not growing up to be 'Tina'. I tried in every way to please them, to be someone they would be happy with. A daughter they could be proud of . . . . could love!

ROBERT

I'm sure your parents loved you.

TINA

No, they loved the girl that they hoped I would grow up to be the slender, beautiful, popular, belle of the ball, blue-eyed blond.

ROBERT

You could be a blond. Anyone can.

TINA

No, blonds have to be skinny. There's nothing uglier than a fat blond. Blond hair is reserved for the skinny. Unless, of course, you were born with it, in which case, unfortunately, you're stuck with it. No, you cannot change to blond, if you're a big girl. People just look at you . . . . like . . . . 'Don't even try!'.

ROBERT

People are cruel sometimes. But I never meant to be . . . . if I ever was. Was I . . . . ever? Cruel, I mean?

TINA

No, Robert, you are . . . were the kindest person I ever met. And I will always cherish . . . the nice little things you did for me . . . . the gifts you gave me, the roses . . . . the sex . . . YOU . . . I'll always cherish your memory, the things we did together.

ROBERT

I never loved anyone but you. And I loved you from day one. (he stands and walks to behind her) Your size did not matter to me. You're intelligent, kind and thoughtful, fun to be with, and great in bed. How could I not love you? How could anyone not love you? (he moves to behind the tombstone, and disappears from view)

TINA

Then, why did you have to leave me? I don't know what I'll do now. I know that no one else will ever . . . . well, you know, (she turns and walks to beside the grave) And I would never want anyone else, anyway, (she walks away to stage left, stops and looks back) By the way, your scent is still in your clothes. I smell you every time I open the closet door. I hope it never goes away. It's like I'll always have part of you with me. I know that's weird but then I'm a weird person, I'm a fat girl.

A BABY IN ORANGE

Character: Emma, a young woman dressed in orange.

Emma enters from stage right. She is tall, slender. She is wearing a wide-brimmed hat (perhaps with flowers or feathers), two strings of beads down to her waist. She has on a knit dress or skirt which is above her knees. Her very high heels are the exact shade of orange as all other elements of her ensemble. She could be a model . . . . or a hooker. She holds a bouquet of orange flowers.

EMMA

I haven't grieved yet. I should grieve . . . I suppose. Someone should. Although I'm not too sure about that. When I go, I don't want nobody crying over me. I hope no one even notices when I go. And probably nobody will, because nobody noticed when I came into this world. My mama was well aware of it for a few hours. All my dad said was, "another bitchy little girl . . . damn!" I was the last of six. Mama didn't say much of anything, I guess. She just died. Dad left. That's about all my sisters told me about mom and dad. Someone should have been there to say . . . oh, I don't know . . . maybe, "She's going to be another Elle McPherson or another Julia Roberts or another Marilyn Van Saint . . . .", but nobody said any such predictions. And I can't remember much being said to me as I grew up . . . . except, "Shut your fucking mouth!", so that's what I did. For sixteen years. Then I met him. (she indicates a grave) He taught me how to walk, (she walks like a trained model across downstage) He taught me how to talk . . . and when not to talk. He taught me how to eat in really fine restaurants. He bought me expensive clothes, and sometimes, he would let me pick them out . . . . you know . . . . select them. He was a good man. He was good to me. He just couldn't teach me how to love. I don't hate. No, I don't hate nobody. But I don't really love nobody either, (she turns to look at the grave). However, I have come to pay my respects, (to the audience) Not that I respected him I don't respect nobody either, (to the grave) I miss you. Thanks for leaving me the money, (she moves to behind the stone.) I'm sorry about saying I didn't respect you. I shouldn't have said that. Maybe I feel at least THAT for you. I wish I could be sure that I feel something . . . . for you or any of the others, (she walks back to the audience downstage) If I thought I could love a baby, I'd have myself one. And if I did love it if I COULD love it . . . . I would with all my heart, day and night, every day and every night. But I could never take that chance. Because I might not even feel love for a baby . . . . and it's a sad thing when a baby ain't loved, (she bows her head to her shoulder and embraces herself for a beat, then she slowly walks offstage right, looking at the orange flowers she is still holding in front of her.)

A DEADLY AFFAIR

Characters: Laura is in her mid-forties. She looks a bit bedraggled, but has been beautiful. She is well-dressed.
Kent, at forty-nine, is still great-looking in a good suit.

LAURA

(she has walked on unobtrusively while preceding character is still on stage. She is standing beside Kent's grave. Kent appears as preceding character exits, and she places flowers on the grave. He does not look at them) I didn't know. I just didn't know. Why didn't you explain it all to me. It's not my fault. At least not ALL my fault. You were partly to blame, and, of course, so was Melissa. I think that John should share the blame also. Well, of course, HE should! He's the one who I can hardly say that word . . . I try not to even THINK that word.

KENT

SHOT! That's the word, Laura. Or were you thinking, "Killed"? "Murdered"? Which one, Laura?

LAURA

All of them! They sound so . . . . cold . . . . and mean!

KENT

They are cold and mean, Laura, "killed" is a cold, mean word, Laura. So is "death".

LAURA

Well, "life" can be cold and mean, too I don't mean just the word, but living it can be awfully cold and mean. Look at what's happened to me.

KENT

You are the only one unscathed in this whole sordid mess.

LAURA

Oh, I was scathed all right! If that is a word. Is "scathed" a word, Kent. I didn't get to go off to college like you did!

KENT

You chose not to go. You sought your fortune otherwise.

LAURA

Well, for my part, I just want you to know that I am sorry, (she places flowers on his tombstone. He walks around to look at them, then back up to her) And I want you to understand.

KENT

Understanding doesn't give me back my life nor my love. It doesn't give me back Melissa.

LAURA

Well, I lost her, too, you know!

KENT

What do you mean?

LAURA

As soon as John's trial was over, she left. She didn't even say "Good-bye". Her last words to me were, "I never want to see you again, mother." Then she just walked to her car, the new sports car I gave her for Christmas, and drove away. She didn't even look back.

KENT

I think that is the treatment that you deserved.

LAURA

I deserved YOU, Kent. I was the first to love you the first to MAKE love with you how many years ago? You left me without saying good-bye. Now, you've left me again . . . and this time you're gone . . . forever! And John, when they took him away, he just walked out of the court room without ever looking at me. The only three people I ever loved left me without even looking back to say (she starts to cry) goodbye. No, NO! Whatever I did, I don't deserve to live with this the rest of my life. All I ever did was to love. I loved TOO much, I guess, because when you came back after all those years, I felt the same love for you . . . . the same passion . . . . that I had for you the day you left to go off to college. And then, when you came back to me . . . .

KENT

But I didn't come back to you, Laura. I met your daughter when she was a student in my Science Class. I had no idea she was YOUR daughter until she took me home to meet her parents. I'm sorry you misunderstood my reason for being there.

LAURA

What else was I to think? When Melissa called me from the University to tell me that she was bringing home someone special, I thought it would be a nice young man that she had met. Then, when it was YOU, I thought she had learned about US you know, about our having been lovers before you went away to college. I thought perhaps you realized that she was my daughter, and that you had told her about us.

KENT

Oh, sure! Like I would consider coming home with her to meet your husband! Besides, I made it clear to you when I left, that it was over, and that I would never come back.

LAURA

I didn't believe you. I really tried to forget you, Kent, but I didn't believe that you could walk away from me like you never loved me at all. I married John, a man thirty years older than myself, just two months after you left me . . . . just to hurt you.

KENT

Perhaps hurting me was one reason. His having ten million dollars in the bank might have been another reason.

LAURA

It was a strong incentive.

KENT

Laura, I made it clear to you as soon as I saw that Melissa's mother was YOU, that I had not come back to you. As soon as I realized that you were of the impression that I had come back to start back where you and I left off, I told you that it was Melissa that I loved.

LAURA

I just couldn't believe it. And I still can't believe that you ever got over me, any more than I got over you.

KENT

I didn't . . . . not completely . . . but I had to go on to college. I couldn't NOT go. Then I met someone else then someone else . . . . many someone else-s through the years. But, no, I never forgot what we had years ago.

LAURA

I knew it! So, it wasn't all my fault. I knew that you still loved me that night you could not resist me. I felt sorry for Melissa, but I wanted you so desperately . . . . and you were mine first.

KENT

You're just trying to make me take part of the guilt, to relieve your own conscience. I never should have gone to your house that night, but you lied to me, Laura. You told me that Melissa and John would be there, and that it was a dinner party for me.

LAURA

I'm so sorry. But I knew if I could see you alone, that I would be able to find out the truth . . . . and I did . . . I found out that you still wanted me the way I wanted you. I asked Melissa to visit her grandmother overnight, and I thought that John was in Atlanta. I didn't know that he had missed his flight.

KENT

Still, I could have left as soon as I arrived to find that we would be alone.

LAURA

But you didn't! You wanted it to happen as much as I did!

KENT

Maybe I did. But I sure didn't want John to walk in on us with that pistol!

LAURA

It was the worse night of my entire life!

KENT

It was the LAST night of my life!

LAURA

I know. I'll never get over it. I'm so sorry . . . . Did it hurt?

KENT

(he finds that funny) The first one hurt like hell! But I barely felt the ones that followed.

LAURA

I regret all the pain that I have caused. And I dread all the heartache I have to live with the rest of my life. I am sure that, of all of us, it is I who has suffered the most pain of all. I am the most . . . . scathed . . . . of all. (she faces the audience, and he disappears behind the headstone) Well, I'm going on an extended vacation to try to recover from all this, (she turns back to find that he is gone) I just wanted to say . . . Kent? . . . . Kent? Damn! Just like before! Why do people always leave me without saying "good-bye"? (she brushes a leaf off the headstone and slowly exits)

A GIRL NAMED REBECCA

Characters: Rebecca, sixteen years old, long blond hair, 1900's attire.

Edward, young man, early twenties, fashionable suit with carnation in lapel.

REBECCA

(she is sixteen years old. She is dead. She has unusually long hair, beautiful, void of "make-up" except for stage purposes to enhance her very bright face. She is in period costume, 1900's. She walks from behind tombstone to down stage center. She is speaking to herself and above, although to, the audience as well) Another decoration day and nobody came. Not one person has ever come to pay respect. I guess I have to face the fact that everyone lost respect for me after what I did. But I should think that after eighty years, someone might forgive me. It does seem that true love deserves some degree of forgiveness. And I did truly love him, even if he did marry Lucy Belle two months after that horrible fire at the hotel. I still don't know how he got out alive. I couldn't find him in all that smoke, and with all the yelling and noise, I know he couldn't hear me calling for him. I should have jumped from the window, but by the time I realized that he wasn't in the room, it was too late I just couldn't breathe anymore, (she walks back to tombstone, then looks back to audience) Mama couldn't come to the funeral. She was so distraught . . . . she never quite recovered. Maybe I should have listened to mama and papa, but I did so love him. Seems like he could have waited a year or two before he married Lucy Belle, (she walks behind tombstone and freezes)

EDWARD

(Edward walks from stage left and looks at names on tombstones until he finds Rebecca's. He stops directly in front of grave, his back to the audience.) Rebecca Mathison . . . . born 1904 . . . died 1920. So there really was a 'Rebecca', and she was only sixteen when it happened.

REBECCA

I don't remember you. Should I know you? (a beat) Of course not! You were not even born when I lived . . . . nor when I died. Who are you? Why did you come looking for my grave?

EDWARD

(He walks to beside the grave, but is really talking to the audience.) I'm Edward Kilgore. My great-grandfather was James Martin. My grandfather used to tell me about a girl of whom his father, my great-grandfather, spoke often. My grandfather was certain that his father loved her very much, (She walks to opposite side of grave. They look directly at each other) and he was sure that he never got over losing you in the fire. On his death bed, it was your name he called with his last breath. He said he was coming to you.

REBECCA

Well, he must have been laid to rest elsewhere. And besides, it's different here. It doesn't matter who you loved before. Everyone is loved the same here. I'm sure he must have been buried beside Lucy Belle.

EDWARD

Oh, yes, she died giving birth to her eleventh child . . . . years before my great-grandfather died. He married again . . . a widow with eight kids, and then they had a set of twins together. Well, I just wanted to come to pay my respects. (He pulls a carnation from his coat lapel.) Here. I want you to have this carnation. You might have been my great-grandmother, you know that is, if you had not died.

Well, I'll go now. (He walks away, stage left. She returns to behind stone.)

REBECCA

Eleven children . . . . eight more . . . . twins. One should never question death.

NARRATOR

(Preacher Mason enters stage left as soon the last character exits. The singing has stopped.) Well, everyone has gone home. Decoration Day is a good thing. It's time for people to come to pay their respects, but it's more than that. It's a time for some to come and say things they wish they had said before it was too late. Some come to say that they are sorry for what they did say and wish that they had not said. Some come to say, "I miss you." Some come to say, "I love you." Some come to say "I'm sorry." Some say, "I'll soon follow you." Others speak with a vengeful heart. And some just come to say . . . . "Good-bye."

THE END

A WALK IN THE MEADOW

BY
ROBERT BERTRAND

A WALK IN THE MEADOW

The "meadow", as Caledonia was want to call the slightly, sloping outcropping in the wooded area behind the house where she raised five children, sometimes yielded beautiful yellow daisies, purple violets, a variety of unidentifiable wild rose vines with small pink roses which profusely covered large spots about the fence that bordered the area openness from the sudden deep-green of the pine trees that formed a backdrop on the edge of her property. The old dilapidated fence of rotting boards, barbed wire and old posts, which stood like gray ghosts during moon-lit nights, no longer served a purpose. Not because it was incapable of keeping quadrupedal, domesticated animals enclosed, but because there were no longer any left to be kept on her property. Cows, mules, horses and pigs had not been utilized for food, nor labor for many years. There were still chickens, ducks, geese and turkey, here and there, pecking around the yard of the house and sometimes about the meadow.

"I'm surprised that you came. I mean, that you are the first one to arrive." Caledonia said to her youngest son, Daniel.

"Don't you mean that you are surprised that I came at all, Mama?" He asked with a hint of sarcasm.

"No. I knew you'd come, but I thought you'd wait until the last minute of the last day." His mother answered. "Of the five of you, I thought you'd be the last to arrive." The two of them, mother and son, sat in rocking chairs on the front porch overlooking the meadow. After several minutes, Caledonia said, "They come more frequently, now, and they stay longer than they use to, it seems."

"Who? The other kids?" Daniel asked.

"Oh. Hell, no. I'm talking about the problems, the kinds that demand attention and some concentration. Time was when I'd of give a problem 20 minutes worth of my concern, then move on with life." She answered.

"At our expense?" He asked.

"Sometimes, maybe."

"What has changed. What caused you to begin to give more thought to problems that come up in life, and to remember that we *all* have them. God didn't just single you out to be the chosen one to have problems." Daniel's words might have been a bit harsh, but his tone was decently respectable.

"Well, as I grew older I began to think life is too short and damnation is too long for me to ignore some . . . . some things."

"In other words, guilt sat down on the lap where we used to wish to sit, and would not get up. So, you realized that you had a conscious." So much for respect! He did not feel like being honorable just now.

"I'm not a psychologist. It doesn't pay to analyze too deeply." She responded.

"Do you have *any* regrets, Mama?" Daniel asked.

"About what?" She turned her gaze from the meadow to the young man's eyes.

"If you have to ask, then that is an answer to my question, and it covers the situation quite completely."

"Daniel, if you regret life, you stop living it. Regret is an abomination. And it has not been easy to cling onto the minuteness, the thin skin of life I had left after he died." Caledonia said, in her defense.

"It was the same life you always had, before he died. You never tried to change it."

His mother replied, "I never said I wanted to change it. And if I had wanted to, how do you think I could have made any changes? Wants can bring on great disappointments."

"He left you some money. You could have left this miserable place." Caledonia tried to slap his face, but missed because she could not reach him from her chair, and she slapped the post of his rocker instead.

"I might have been a bad mother, a miserable person living a miserable life, as you seem to think, but this place is not miserable, never has been. It has been my fortress, my place to hide away from a world I never asked to be in. Never wanted to be in."

"Not even when you and dad were in love and?" Daniel asked, stopping short.

"Who said we were in love? I don't remember *him* ever telling anybody he loved me. Did he ever tell you he loved me? Did he ever tell you he loved *you?*"

Daniel did not have to ponder that question. After awhile he said, "He tried to get you to go with him. I heard discussions about it more than once. He asked you to leave here and be with him."

"I didn't want to go. I would have gone with him, but he did not try hard enough to get me to go. Not hard enough to convince me that he really wanted me to go." She responded, looking far beyond the meadow above the distant tree tops where the sun was still quite bright. There were still hours before darkness would fall across the meadow almost the minute that the sun would drop far beyond the green pines which would become black even in the moonlight. There was still time for the others to come.

"Do you really believe that he was not sincere when he would come back home to you, and ask you to go with him and live in the city?" Daniel asked.

"I should go to the city and live among people I didn't know, didn't understand? No. I would have been inadequate. He would have been embarrassed of me. His highflying friends would have had me taking in their washing and scrubbing their floors."

"You could have acquired an education, if you had gone to the city! It's your own fault that you didn't! Dad gave you money."

"It was my *choice*, not my *fault!*" She got up from her chair and walked to the kitchen in order to put the kettle on to make her afternoon tea. Daniel followed her to the kitchen and sat at the table, which served as a "cook table" as well as the "eating table". There was no dining room in the house. The meals were cooked and eaten in the same room. "After I spent all the money my daddy left me, on *his* college expenses, I had to sell eggs, butter, hogs whatever I had, so that he could finish his last year in college.

After he got the MBA, we were to be married and I would begin my studies."

"So, why didn't you? What stopped you?" Daniel was curious.

"He would bring money home to me, get me pregnant again, and there was no talk of me going to college, nor of marriage." She explained.

"It was not all his fault. You are an intelligent woman, Mama. What is more, you are a strong woman. You could have made choices."

"I said it was my choice. I saved all the money he gave me to send the five of you to get your educations. After he died, there wouldn't have been enough money left for you to go to college, had you not gotten scholarships. I even sold a small piece of the property to get you through graduate school"

"Didn't you ever want to do something else, be *someone?* "

"I am someone! I'm me! Caledonia Thacker! A woman who had five babies she didn't want, but who loved her five babies more than anything in this world. I wanted to be who I was, who I am, your mother!" Then, she added, "I love you . . . all of you."

"I'm sorry, Mama." Daniel spoke softly. "What I meat was, didn't you ever have dreams of your own, dreams of something you wanted to do?" Then after another brief silence, "Of course you did! Everybody has a dream they want to pursue."

"I figure I've made some great achievements. I raised five children, threw them into college whether they wanted to go or not, not even giving a consideration as to whether they wanted to go or not. That should have been my contribution to society. If it has not made the world a better place, it's not my fault. When each of you got out of high school, I put you all out and into college. I had done all I could do to prepare you for a world where you would meet and compete with the unfair, backstabbing bastards and bitches you would have to deal with, or maybe even become!"

They walked back into the parlor, after finishing their tea. They sat there for a long while without speaking.

"I accomplished something else, too." Caledonia said suddenly. "I learned how to be happy alone, after you all were gone. I, too, got an education. I educated myself. The town library is full of books, most of which I've read. I learned a lot about human nature by observing life around me. The farm animals, the wild ones too. The birds, insects and other creatures I meet during my evening walks in the meadow. Even the occasional snake I meet up with they taught me to never trust my luck with anyone, not with any creature . . . . walking or crawling . . . . , not even nature itself. Love it, just don't trust it. A wisp of a cloud can become a deadly storm in minutes. Let sleeping dogs lie, and move the hell out of their territory quietly and quickly. And I don't mean the quadrupedal ones; it's the two-legged ones I'm talking about. They are the ones that hurt you the most."

"Mama, listen to yourself. You've become a bitter, old lady." Great concern was in his voice. A tear was on each cheek.

"Another choice I made, I suppose." She responded.

Later in the evening, when it seemed obvious that none of the others were coming, they went into the kitchen again. Caledonia took two TV dinners from the refrigerator and put them into the microwave oven.

"Mama, those can't be good for you. Let me fix you some dinner."

"For years I ate good food. Like they said on TV. You know, fresh fruits, fresh vegetables, all the right things the TV news would tell you was good for you. Well, they should have told my heart that. Three stints and an imminent date with death tells me they don't know a damn thing about what's good for anybody." She said.

She pours glasses of milk. I have tea, or wine, if you don't still drink milk." She said. "It's soy milk, good for your heart! I have to buy stuff at the store now. I don't have a cow anymore. Go on out to the porch. We'll eat out where it's cool. I'll bring our trays out in a few minutes."

Outside, hesitantly, he asked, "Mama, did the doctor tell you how long?"

"Who can believe that lying bastard?" Her face turned from ordinary seriousness to an expression of fear. "I figure a month. Maybe just one more day."

"I could take you back with me, you know."

"Not a chance. I'd just be in the way. I wouldn't want to hinder Charles and you from doing anything whatever it is that you do."

They sit quietly and finish their TV dinners. Daniel finally spoke. "It's been a long time since you went into the city to stay awhile. I really want you to come."

"Nothing I can get there that I need. That I can't get here at the store in town.

I remember once I went to the city, planning to stay awhile. Your dad asked me to come. I took the bus. I was pretty back then. He wanted to show me off to his friends. He took me to a party. A company party. My dress was new. My make-up was not done well. I must have looked a sight!" She laughs. "I think his friends thought I was a two-bit hooker he'd picked up on the way to the party. He never invited me to come back again." Her smile went away. "I had good hair. If I had anything remotely resembling a dream, it was to advertise hair products on TV."

"And you would have looked great on TV."

There was silence again. Caladonia took the lunch containers back to the kitchen, and then she returned. She sat on the front steps with her arms around her knees. "I want to be buried here. Well, not here on the farm. But there's a little church down the road, you remember it, I took you there a few times. The church is old. It's little, but the cemetery is big. There's plenty of room, and the plots don't cost anything. That's where your grand-parents and other relatives were buried. You and the others should be laid to rest, when your time comes, near your dad, wherever it is that his family put him."

"Mama, I don't want . . . . I'm not ready to discuss this now, not tonight." The two of them walk into the parlor. They picked up magazines and newspapers to look at. Daniel saw her glance through the window, to look down the road. He knew that she was still hopeful that the others would come. He knew that his brothers and sisters would not show up.

"Daniel." She called.

"Yes, Mama."

"We do need to talk about it. Soon. Not tonight, but soon."

"We will." After a beat, he said, "Mama, did we ever pick dewberries together when I was a little boy?"

"You remember that? Sure. We'd go out across the meadow and pick gallons of dewberries, and later in the summer, there would be blackberries, too." She said.

"And flowers. Lots of flowers." Daniel said, smiling.

"Yes! Lots of flowers. All kinds of wild flowers." She looked at her son, pleased that he had these memories. "I'm so glad you remember. I thought I was the only one who had all those good memories. Sometimes I even dream about those days. And the nights, too. We'd sit out on the porch and listen to the crickets and frogs."

Excitedly, Daniel said, "And sometimes we would sing."

"Yes, we'd sing, too! We sounded worse than the bullfrogs. But it was so much fun." There was a sudden silence between them. Then she said, "But that was before you started spending the summers with your father in the city. You didn't like going with him at first, but then you met Charles. Then, as time went by and you were growing up, you didn't want to come back here when the summers were over."

"I'm sorry that I did not come to see you more often."

"Oh, there was nothing here to interest you. Nor any of the others either. I wonder when they will come. The others. You shouldn't have to take care of . . . . this business alone." His mother said.

"They're not coming, Mama. They want to, I'm sure, but they thought that I should come. They have their families, you know, the children . . . . and the house here is so little . . . ."

"I'm not so sure they wanted to come." She said firmly.

"You know that Matt and Mark are busy running Dad's company. Sarah is teaching summer school courses at the university. She couldn't possibly take time out just now. Jean is in Europe. She took a group of young people from her church, an obligation she made months ago."

"So, you got stuck with the duty of . . . . taking care of my final business."

"Mama, I came because I wanted to come. I came because I love you."

She looked at her son, her youngest child. "That's good. Regardless of how much truth is in it or the lack thereof, those are good words to hear at this particular time in my fragile life."

"Mama, you look tired. Why don't you lie down and get some rest. Tomorrow we'll talk about what needs to be done after you . . . ." He could not say it.

"Yes, I'll lie down for awhile. And when I wake up, we can go for a walk in the meadow."

Four Old Whores From Sycamore Street

By
Robert Bertrand

FOUR OLD WHORES FROM SYCAMORE STREET

(HORTENSE, BESSIE, KATE AND LUCILE)

The room is dimly lighted with a chandelier and two side lamps, in the Tiffany style. The wall paper was Chinese red with roses in a lighter shade of red (though not pink), and the doors were a shade of green which Hortense had seen in some Chinese art. Furniture, set close together, a bit crowded with two love seats, two matching chairs in the same ashy rose color as the rose blossoms in the wall paper, were adorned with gold fringe around the bottom edges of the antiquated pieces. Small marble-top tables were placed snugly in between the pieces of furniture. On these were the two Tiffany style lamps as well as an assortment of cheap French and Chinese figurines. The room was utterly gaudy, but in the best taste of tawdriness. Despite the harshly overdone colors and aged furnishings, it was uniquely cozy and inviting. It was obvious upon entering the room, that cleanliness and pride was a factor in the character of the person who resided in this well-kept little house on Sycamore Street.

Hortense straightened a fold in the heavy, red velvet drapes over one of the two windows on the side wall, windows that would have revealed a lovely little courtyard with a variety of blooming plants and a small fountain of water flowing into a little fish pool. There was a faded-green bird bath, too. Blue birds and other feathered friends could almost always be seen when Hortense would peak beyond the velvet drapes. The drapes were never opened. Sunlight would fade the color in the furniture fabric, which was the same as the drapes. The drapes, however, were heavily lined with white linen in order to reflect the sunlight away. Hortense turns on two lamps in order that she might make a last minute check for dust on the marble table tops. Of course, there is not a speck of dust to be seen. Over the fireplace mantle, there is a picture of flowers, which Hortense herself had probably painted. She straightened it, stood away and looked to see if it was in its perfect position. There was another picture on the opposite wall. It was an enlargement of a picture of four young women dressed in rather gaudy clothing. The picture was appealing due to the innocent, sweet smiles on the faces of the four young women. Despite innocence and sweetness, the smiles expressed happiness, fun-loving naughtiness. The young women in the picture were Hortense, and her co-workers, Bessie, Kate and Lucile. The four were to see each other again for the first time in twenty-five years. Hortense was expecting them to arrive soon.

The first to arrive was Bessie. Hortense hurried to the door to welcome her in.

"Bessie!" They hug, stand back, still holding hands, and look at each other.

"Hortense McCalister, you look great!" Bessie said.

"You, too, Bessie." Hortense exclaimed.

"Oh, Hor, you know that I never looked great. With my looks, I had to be great at what I did, otherwise I never could have made it in the business!" They both laugh. "Am I the first to arrive? The others are coming, aren't they?"

"Yes, Kate is flying in from New York tonight, and Lucile will come by Greyhound tomorrow." Hortense said.

"Oh, that Kate. She should not have paid for a flight. She could just have mounted her broom and flown right on down to Birmingham."

"Now, Bessie, don't you go starting any mess with Kate!" Hortense warned.

"I don't know what you're talking about, dear Hortense." Bessie teased.

"Oh, yes, you do! I remember all the fights you two would get into." Hortense nonchalantly picks up a small framed picture from a table and attempts to slip into the small drawer of the table. "Especially that last one just before we all split."

"What are you hiding there. Let me see that picture!" Bessie has it in her hands before Hortense could hide it away in the table drawer. "Why, you have his picture." She frowns slightly, curiously. "How did you get this?" She reads a message written on the front of the picture: 'To Polly, with love!' He wrote your real name."

"It doesn't matter how I got it." Hortense took the picture from Bessie and placed it in the drawer of the table. "Come on out to the kitchen. I'll make us a cup of tea."

"I'd rather have some of your delicious cold, sweet lemonade! No body could make sweet lemonade like you, Hor. Remember how our men used to like your sweet lemonade? Especially *him*", Bessie said, indicating, with a swish of her hand, the picture which was just placed in the table drawer.

"Sorry. I don't have any lemons. I have not made lemonade in years. He preferred hot tea in his later years." Hortense said.

"Oh. Really. In his *later* years?" Bessie was curious, but she let it drop. "It used to be so hot in this little place. But now it's air conditioned. When did you come back and buy our . . . . this place?"

"A long time ago. I don't remember exactly when." She is heating tea in the microwave oven.

"Oh, I see." Bessie walks back into the parlor and looks around at the furniture, as though she had not really noticed it upon her first arrival. "The same furniture. Eastlake. The same old chandelier. Why, you must have come back real soon after we closed our 'business' down. Or, rather, after it was closed down for us."

Hortense enters the room with a tray. "Here is our tea. Come, sit down. I want you to tell me everything. Don't leave out anything from the day we walked out of here 'til today."

Bessie looks up at the chandelier. She said, "Trust me, Hor, it's not that interesting. But I'll hit the low spots and leave out the highs. To tell about them would be too shocking for you, and too sad for me." They drink their tea while Bessie talks. "After we left here, I went to Atlanta to visit my aunt who told me that my mama was dying. She talked me into going to see her before she died. Big mistake! Nothing had changed. She still thought that I should have gone to college rather than gone to prostitution. The only thing that had changed was that I agreed with her. But we argued anyway. She died. I had a house. My last years in the house here were not so lucrative. You know I never was pretty, never was 'first choice'. So, I now had a house in Atlanta, but no money saved up."

"Don't tell me you went back into the business of . . ."

"Oh, no! After all, my best days were in the past. So were my best _nights._ "She smiled, remembering. "Fortunately for me, mama had left my education fund in the bank. It had accumulated quite a bundle. I made mama proud. Albeit belatedly. I went to college. I've been teaching school, kindergarten, for the last twenty years. I'll retire soon. Life's not so bad." They returned to the kitchen and placed the tea tray in the kitchen sink. Hortense proceeds to wash the cups and saucers.

"I'm assuming that you never . . . . well, you know, married." Hortense said, carefully.

"That area, love, marriage, well those were the sad highlights of my life that I was leaving out. No, I never married. Love came and went. Marriage never came. I was never offered money, nor marriage. My college degree did not change my past. I cried a lot and adjusted to life without men, eventually."

They went back into the parlor to sit. Hortense said, "Living alone . . . . I mean, ending up alone . . . . Is not so bad if you have some good memories."

Bessie said, "Well, I have a few. It was fun living here with you girls. And I remember a few good men. I remember him especially. He was fantastic, wasn't he? I guess we all remember him." She looked toward the table drawer where the picture was placed. Then she looked at Hortense's face for some reaction to what she had said.

Hortense did not respond by expression, nor word. "We'll go out to eat when Kate arrives. She should arrive soon."

Bessie said, "You know, I really liked Kate, in spite of her bitchy ways. She always had an attitude about everything, and it was always different from ours."

"Well, our clients really liked her. She was pretty, and she had a natural ability, a talent for pleasing a man."

"She was a natural born whore, that was her talent!" Bessie remarked.

Hortense smiled. "At her prices, you could hardly call her a whore. Considering her high prices, she was a high-priced prostitute. But, I suspect we have all changed as the years have gone by."

"I tried to. But I never seemed to be able to change very much. But you, you, Hortense, you are very different. You've aged in a good way. You have a softness, an elegance about you that I never noticed back then. I think you have become a different kind of person, someone respectable, lady-like, someone to be envied." Bessie sat thinking about Kate. She said, "I guess I was just jealous of her. She was the one who usually was picked by Jean-Pierre. He was so good. And I don't mean just good in bed. He was a good-hearted man. And his looks! Oh, my God, what a hunk. Not to mention the fact that he had a . . ." The doorbell rang.

Hortense was happy that the door bell rang just at that moment. "Oh, that will be Kate!" She rushes to the door. Kate is dressed in an expensive pant suit. Too much jewelry adorned her ears, neck, wrists and fingers. Bessie joins them near the door. There are greetings and hugging exchanged in excitement. "Kate you look marvelous! You haven't changed a bit!" Hortense said. And Bessie even added, "As pretty as ever."

"Yes, I know. Thank you for noticing. I do take care of myself. And you look great Hortense, except you've let your hair go gray. And you look nice, too, Bessie, even with the extra pounds you've put on since I last saw you."

"OK, I take back what I said. You look just as old as we do!" They all laugh, even if Kate did not find it funny.

Hortense said, "I didn't *let* my hair go gray. It just went that way, Kate. I am sixty-seven years old now."

Kate took off her knee-length jacket and handed it to Hortense. She found a wall mirror and touched up her still blond hair. "What have you two old whores been talking about? Me! I am sure."

Bessie, with sarcasm, said, "Still as conceited as ever, always thinking that everything is about you, Kate."

"Well, isn't it?" Kate said. Again they all laugh.

"If you still insist, I guess it is still all about you, Kate." Bessie said, but no one laugh now.

Hortense motioned for all to sit. "Truthfully, we were talking about you. About how you always threw yourself at the richest of our clients."

"Yes, like with that Jean-Pierre guy. You always tried to grab him first, instead of letting him have his pick, make his own choice of which one of us he might want." Bessie said.

Kate said, "Well, after he had had all of us, I was his choice."

Bessie followed up with, "Given a chance, he might have chosen."

Hortense intervened. "Bessie, you promised. All of that is in the past. I invited you all here so that we could remember the good times of the past, and talk about our present-day lives. We just want to catch up on where each of us is, in our lives now."

"Where are we eating? I'm starved. Is there a decent place in Birmingham to find a good meal?" Kate asked.

"Of course. Birmingham has changed during the last twenty-five years, Kate. Even the crime rate has changed, but not for the better!" Hortense said.

"Well, this house certainly has not changed." Kate was looking around at the furniture and the walls. "Neither has Sycamore Street, except perhaps a few more crack houses." They pick up their wraps and purses, and Hortense calls a taxi. Kate said, "Someplace with some atmosphere and excellent food. Price is not problem! I'm paying!" They leave and Hortense closes the door behind them.

*   *   *

The following morning, Hortense insisted on Bessie and her waiting for Kate to wake up before they had breakfast. They were still in their sleeping clothes, sipping coffee, when Kate finally appeared in the kitchen. Kate was fully dress, including make-up. Hortense fixed eggs and other breakfast food while the three of them talked.

Kate said, "Too bad that poor Lucile had to hop a bus all the way from Little Rock. If only I had known, I could have paid for her flight here to Birmingham."

"Do you really think that Lucile would have accepted your charity, Kate?" Bessie asked.

"Well, I don't see why not? Why would you say that? If the poor woman can't afford to fly, she should not have too much pride to enjoy a free flight." Kate said.

Hortense saw that it was time to intervene. "It doesn't matter. She'll be here soon anyway. And she might have preferred the scenic bus trip, rather than flying."

"Sure! The scenic route between Arkansas and Alabama! Really, Hortense, no one in her right mind would prefer a bus, oh, well, she *is* from Arkansas." Kate retorted.

"And where were you from, Kate, before you lassoed that wealthy Texan and ended up in New York City with all his money?" Bessie asked.

"I lived about here and there . . . . all over."

"In other words, you never had a home." Bessie looked at her eye-to-eye. That is the way it was with Bessie. Always straight forward, always saying exactly what she thought, regardless of consequences. "And how did you get all that man's money, anyway, I mean with you being a slut and everything? Divorce?"

"No. Death." Kate said, sadly.

"You killed him?" Bessie was quick to ask.

Hortense spoke again, "Bessie, that's uncalled for. You've said enough."

"No. It's OK. I remember Bessie's mouth from twenty-five years back. I shouldn't have expected that she would have changed, except for looking quite a bit older." Kate sipped her hot coffee. "He died happy, in bed."

"So, you did kill him." Bessie quipped.

Kate ignored her implication. "I got most of his money. Those daughters of his were real bitches. But I had a good lawyer. He agree with me that trophy wives are deserving, too."

Hortense could not resist saying, "At forty something, I hardly think you could fall under the category of 'trophy wife', Kate."

"Well, he was more than twice my age! The important thing is that I made him happy for three long months, and he made me happy for the rest of my life!"

"By dying!" Bessie said.

"No, by leaving me the money when he did die." Kate said.

Hortense urged her to tell them more. "Then what, Kate? What have you been doing all these years as the merry widow, after you got out of Dodge?"

"It was Houston. I moved to New York and enjoyed life. With the money I had, men were always in my life . . . . not like when I was here, I mean I do not need money from them. I never lost my good looks. I've been fortunate to be one of those few people on God's green Earth whose beauty only becomes enhanced with age."

"I'll have to admit, you were the pretty one. Bessie, Lucile and I were chosen only when you were already busy with another client, that is if he didn't have time to wait for you." Hortense said.

"That's a matter of opinion. Mainly, Kate's opinion. We all had our regulars. I had quite a nest egg saved up when we closed the operation." Bessie stated, and Hortense knew it was a lie. She had already told her that she had gone to Atlanta without money.

"Yes, Bessie, it is my opinion that I am pretty." Kate said. "That's one of the qualities that a woman has to have if she is going to stay pretty . . . . I mean, she has to have the opinion that she is pretty. It is as important as having pretty eyes, or good legs, nice complexion . . . . when a woman begins to think she is not pretty anymore, she isn't. It's like with a man. When he thinks he can't do it anymore, he's soon going to lose it. My attitude about my looks is something I learned from French women. A French woman can have a face like a dog, but if she thinks she's prettier than every other woman, that she is unique, and if she does something to herself to make herself different from the rest, well, men like that. It can be in the way she sits, the way she stands, the way she walks . . . . just in the way she flutters her lashes as she looks up, or the way she places a flower in her hair, or on the hip of her well-fitted dress, of the best fabric, of course . . . . that's what makes a woman maintain her beauty."

"Thanks for the French lesson, Kate." Bessie quipped.

Hortense asked, "After your wealthy Texan died, did you ever consider marrying again?"

"Oh, sure! I had proposals, considered some, but in the final analysis well, let's face it: once a whore, always a whore. And we were all whores! I just didn't want marriage. Why marry the bull, if you can get the or whatever the saying is."

"Kate, I think you are wrong. I think you can leave the business and put it behind you so far into the past that you seldom ever think about it." Hortense argued. "Take Bessie for example, she has become a respectable school teacher."

"That's nice. An honorable profession I hear. But I will bet my fortune that if Jean-Pierre should come by right now and proposition her, she'd flop in bed before you could count two-bits. Right, Bessie?" Kate smiled sweetly.

Bessie said, "I haven't thought of Jean-Pierre in years." She looks at Hortense and then to the table drawer where his picture was placed earlier. "Don't tell me you're still jealous because he did not prefer you."

"No!" Kate was quick to respond. Then, for some reason, she felt it necessary to follow on with this line of conversation. She could not stop herself. She could not have them think that she did not win Jean-Pierre. "As a matter of fact, I dumped *him* years ago. You know, he followed me to Houston, then to New York. He still wants me. Calls me now and then. But I moved on. I do not avail myself to him."

Hortense began, "Kate! I need to tell you . . . ." Again the doorbell interrupted a discussion. They know that it must be Lucile.

All at once, more hugs and greetings. Lucile was the youngest of the four women. She had not been a common-looking girl at all, but her back-woodsy ways had not helped her as far as making big tips when they ran the house. At this time in her life, she actually appeared to be the oldest of the four. Lucile, too, was amazed at how well preserved the old house was. She said, "Hortense, how did you ever arrange to reserve this old place for the week-end? My God, you sluts have aged! You all look like hell!" They all laugh except for Kate.

"Speak of yourself, Lucile! Men still find me attractive."

"Well, Kate, judging from that expensive outfit you're wearing, and all that bling bling, I can guess you can well afford to pay them to say that."

Bessie is quick to add, "That's a switch isn't it. She used to get paid for it, and now she has to pay them!"

"I do not!" Kate snapped. "I'd never lower my standards to pay a man for . . . . anything!"

Bessie would not be outdone. "So, you're saying men lowered their standards by paying for you!"

"Bessie, you have not changed at all. You are still the bitch you always were." Kate said.

"I had to be one in order to keep you in your place. Your high-tone antics never impressed me one bit. You were a prostitute just like the rest of us were, and maybe you still are." Bessie said.

"Actually, she was the biggest prostitute, because she always had more clients and got paid more!" Lucile said.

Bessie said, "We all did well enough. We all paid our share of the rent on this house. Plus, I had enough money to go back to school, get my degree and move on to a respectable living teaching special children."

"Are you suggesting that the rest of us are not living respectable lives?" Kate asked.

"Not exactly 'suggesting' it. Just guessing about you in particular." Bessie said.

Hortense said, "Bessie, we are here to reminisce, not to accuse. Besides, if Kate is still prostituting, it's her own business."

Bessie is expressing long-buried anger. "It's my guess that it's not her 'business' but her habit. I doubt if she can call herself an honorable prostitute. I think she's a plain whore, with money for as many toys as she wants!"

While the unkind words of this conversation were being hurled about the room, Hortense had been busy going and coming through from the kitchen where she has set the table for four. "Girls, I have prepared one of our favorite meals from years passed. Pot roast, baked potatoes, salad and apple pie. Bessie, come help me set out the food." Hortense takes her to the kitchen before the argument would become more heated.

They are seated at the table. Lucile said, "So you are in New York. You always said you would get there someday."

"And very comfortably so, I may say." Kate replied.

Lucile asked, "Is it as great as you thought it would be?"

"Even better! I have a wonderful life. Fine apartment, the theatre, the opera, cute young men to escort me to the finest restaurants." Kate takes out a cigarette and lights it before Hortense notices. "And you, Lucile? What about you. You have not told us anything about yourself. What could you possibly find of any interest in Little Rock, Arkansas?"

Just before she takes another puff from her smoke, Hortense gingerly, but with determination, plucks the cigarette from Kate's fingers, dips the lit end into Kate's drink and takes it to the trash can. She does not say a word. Neither does Kate.

"Little Rock is not so little, Kate. My life there is not so bad. And I get away sometimes. Like, I get into New York occasionally." She said it with great purpose and attention to enunciation. The words got Kate's full attention.

"Oh. Really? Well you should have called on me when you've been in the city."

Lucile said, "I did!" They stare at each other. Hortense and Bessie look from one to the other. Hortense is placing the last platter of food on the table, wondering where this little discussion is going. Again the four sit at the table. They are all wondering who is going to speak next. Hortense speaks. "We all want to hear about your life in Arkansas, Lucile. Did you ever marry? What kind of work did you do?"

Bessie said, "But we want to hear more about your visits to New York, first." She is intrigued.

Lucile is looking at her plate. But looks up at Kate when she says, "I don't think Kate has told us everything she'd like us to know about her own life, yet."

Kate is firm. "There's no more, Lucile!"

Bessie asks, "Lucile, did you know that Jean-Pierre is still chasing Kate?"

Kate insists, "I did not say he is 'chasing' me, Bessie. I just said that he drops by to see me from time to time. But, like I said, I've moved on. I'm over the little crush I had on him way back then. I'll admit that I once wanted him, and that I even asked him to marry me once. But I met someone with more money and married him instead. And he was not interested in marriage back then, and now well, now, I am not."

Hortense is looking daggers across the table at Kate. Bessie is looking at Hortense. Lucile is looking at Kate.

"OK. About myself." Lucile started. "I went from here straight back to Little Rock, where I had relatives. I was not welcomed by them. Met a guy. Got engaged. Some relative blabbed about my past. Got dumped. Then I went back into the business. I'm still in it. At least part-time. I can still turn the odd trick once in a blue moon. During those years, I met a nice John. He came to town on business frequently. An elderly gentleman, who paid me well for services rendered. After he retired, he'd send me air fare for me to fly into New York City."

"Well." Kate said, "That's all very interesting, Lucile. Now, it is Hortense's turn to share her story."

Lucile glared at Kate. "I have not finished mine yet, Kate!"

Kate snarled, "So, your hick relatives in Arkansas disowned you, you were dumped by some country pumpkin, you've actually been to New York, and now you're still tricking, back in Podunk, Arkansas! Doesn't that tell it all, Lucile?"

Softly, Lucile said, "Yes. For now, that is all."

Bessie said, "Sounds like the best is yet to come." She looks from Lucile to Kate. "And I'm looking forward to hearing the rest."

*　　　*　　　*

After clearing the table, Hortense brought a silver tray of coffee and cookies into the parlor where the other three women sat. Lucile and Bessie were seated on one of the love seats. Kate sat in a chair near them.

Hortense, at the encouragement of the others, said, "There's very little of interest to tell about my life. But then, I find that none of you had much to share which was all that exciting, either." Not really meaning to offend them, she smiles. "I think it is an achievement that Bessie" . . . she has not yet sat down, and she stands looking at Bessie as she begins to pour coffee to pass around to the women "went on to earn a college degree and to contribute to society by becoming a teacher." She takes coffee to Lucile.

"Lucile, it's commendable that, although still single as we all are, now, you make you own way in life. To be independent and not have to rely 'on the kindness of friends', as Blanche would say, is an accomplishment in itself. And, Kate, . . ." She is serving Kate a cup of coffee, when the doorbell rings. "Oh, excuse me while I answer the door."

The seated women are asking: "Who can that be?"; "This time of the night?"; "A gentleman caller?" "Is she still in the business?". All these questions are spoken at the same time.

"Come in, dear." Hortense says at the open door. "I'm so glad you could make it. I want you to meet my dear, old friends. Sit here while I fetch another cup from the kitchen, and then I will introduce you."

All three women look directly at the stunningly handsome young man, in awe and disbelief. Bessie left her seat and walked to the table where the picture is hidden. She took it out of the drawer and compared it with the face of the young man. She put it back into the drawer, just as Hortense re-enters the parlor, and returned to her seat.

Kate said, "Why there is a remarkable resemblance to"

Hortense interrupted with, "Bessie, Lucile and Kate. Girls I want you to meet Jean-Marc, my wonderful, handsome son. He's finishing his doctorals at UAB. I'm so proud of him!"

Jean-Marc said, "Ladies, I am so happy to finally meet you. Mother has spoken so fondly of you all through the years. I can see by the picture that you all were great friends, and you must have had good times together." He is pointing to the enlarged picture of the four women.

"I hope that she did not tell you everything! Tell me you didn't, Hortense!" Bessie pleaded. Light laughter came from them all.

"She spoke fondly of you all. And she has such good memories of each of you. She has spoken of many of the good times you shared together." Jean-Marc said.

Hortense is about to pour her son a cup of coffee. "Oh, no, mother. Thanks, but I have friends waiting. I just wanted to stop by and meet the delightful ladies of whom you have spoken so often." He said., rising from his chair and going to the door. He turned to bow slightly to them and to bid them "good night". He and Hortense went to the door. He said, "It is a pleasure to finally meet you all. I hope your visit is as much fun as your good times from the past were. Good night, ladies." Hortense closed the door behind him and returned to take her cup of coffee to her chair.

"Well, That was a pleasant surprise, Hor." Lucile said.

Kate said, "Surprise, indeed! You never told us that you married. Why have you kept that from us?"

Hortense said, "It just had not come up. I would have told you the truth before you leave."

Bessie spoke, "As much information as we've shared about our lives," She is looking at Kate, "I think the best is yet to come."

The parlor was dark, except for a night light near the floor. Kate entered from the door which leads to the bedrooms. She held her suitcase in one hand, and her travel bag and purse in the other. She walked quietly to the entrance door when Hortense entered from the kitchen door.

Hortense was surprised by seeing Kate in the dark. "Kate? What are you doing?"

"Oh, my God! You scared the crap out of me." Kate had dropped her suitcase.

"Well, you startled me, too What do you mean, leaving like a thief in the night? Should I count the silver?"

"Well, it just seemed to me like it is the best thing to do . . . . under the circumstances.". Kate put her travel bag down on the floor. "I feel like this whole get-to-gather arrangement of yours was just to humiliate me."

"Kate, don't be ridiculous. You get yourself into humiliating situations without the help of others."

Kate sits in one of the chairs. "Your son, obviously he's Jean-Pierre's. He's the spittin' image of his father. When he came through that door, it was like we had stepped back in time twenty-five years. Just for a heart beat, I thought it was Jean-Pierre." They do not speak for a minute. Then Kate continues, "Well, you know that I was lying about Jean-Pierre coming frequently to visit me in New York."

Hortense responded, "Yes. My reason for encouraging all of us to separate and move on with our different lives, was because of Jean-Pierre. The law was not involved in our closing down the 'house'." Hortense came to sit near Kate. "You see, Jean-Pierre and I were in love. He asked me to get rid of you all. He said that if I would stay, that he would buy me this house, and he would live here with me. He did. No, we never married. Jean-Pierre had a wife in Paris, France. He seldom flew back home to see her. She had her own lover, and had no interest in coming to America. Jean-Pierre had businesses here in Atlanta, Birmingham and New Orleans."

Hortense stood, took a tissue to wipe away a tear, and said, as she walked about the room, "When he died, twelve years ago, he left me 'well-fixed' financially.

I had his body flown back to Paris to his wife, for burial. As far as I know, she never knew about me, even if it is not unusual for French men to take a mistress. I told our son the true circumstances. He and I have been to Paris to visit his grave."

"I'm happy for you, Hor. You had the kindest, most generous . . . . and most handsome . . . . not to mention the most well-endowed . . . . man among our clients."

"He was never a client, Kate. We were lovers from the first night he came into this house." Hortense corrected her.

"Well, you turned a common little whorehouse into a loving home, after you threw all of us out. You've had a good life."

Hortense smiled and said, _"And you,_ you've done well yourself."

Again, Kate is preparing to leave. "I might as well tell you the truth. The part about my Texas husband was true, but the money I got was much less than I led you to believe. Those bitch daughters did get most of it. I had enough to purchase a small apartment, continued in the only profession I knew, finally had enough to buy a bigger house which now serves as my headquarters for my business . . . . that being a 'Madam'. Even rich, old men prefer my young girls over me. But I'm doing OK." She picked up her bag from the floor.

Hortense said, "Kate, you're wrong about me wanting to humiliate you. It was just a simple reunion for four old . . . . ladies."

The two hug a last good-bye. "Good bye, Hor. When Lucile tells Bessie about me tomorrow when I'm gone, enjoy the laugh with them. I would not want her to be disappointed, but I won't give her the pleasure of telling on me in my presence." With that said, Kate left the house.

The next morning at the breakfast table, while Hortense is pouring coffee, Bessie said, "The bitch! You mean she just left without telling us goodbye?"

Hortense said, "It was an emergency, and she didn't want to disturb your sleep."

Lucile said, "I think _I_ might be that emergency. Once when I was in New York, I looked her up. Went to her place and found that she was a Madam in her own whorehouse. I was not going to tell you, nor her, but I guess she figured that I knew, and that I would certainly tell you."

Bessie said, "Well, you would have! I would never have let you leave here without sharing what you had learned about her, and I knew that you had found out what her New York life was like!"

"Did we really enjoy this reunion, girls?" Hortense asked.

"I did." Bessie said. "I just wish that Kate had waited and told us all what she told you. If she had, I was willing to forgive her for being such a bitch when we all lived and worked here together."

Lucile said, "I had a son, too." She had not meant to announce it. It just came out suddenly. Looking at the surprise on their faces, she continued. "I gave him up. I mean I let a nice couple adopt him. I could not afford to keep him, and would not have been a fit mother. At least that's what I told myself." There was silence for a moment.

"Well, Hotlanta is calling me home. I'll be leaving on an eleven ten flight." Bessie announced.

This prompted Lucile to say, "And I'll be catching the afternoon 'dog' back to Little Rock. Who knows, maybe I will meet some wealthy, lonely, old man on the bus. Or better still, a young one!" They laugh. Bessie said, "Lucile, wealthy men do not go Greyhound." To this, Lucile responded, "Well, I might as well dream for the best."

Hortense: "Yes. Always dream for the best."

THE END

UP THE HOURGLASS

BY
ROBERT BERTRAND

UP THE HOURGLASS

"The hours pass, but you don't go away. Where did you go? I mean long ago when you left. And why? And why are you back here now? I've called your name so many times, but I never called you. I never asked you to come back, not even once, so why now?"

The room is dark, but it is not night. He was not asleep, but it seemed like a dream. He sat on the edge of the bed and stroked his gray beard. He should have gotten the hair around the sides and back of his head trimmed last week. The top was bald. He wished it would all go away.

He lay back on the bed and re-arranged his pillow. He closed his eyes as the younger man sat in silence in a chair beside the window. "Turn the music down. You always played that damn music too loud." He was not sure whether it was the radio, the TV, or the DVD. It sounded like loud music and voices, too, but it seemed far away. Perhaps it was in another house on another street, or perhaps it was in another year, a long time ago.

The room was still dark, although bright rays of sunlight filtered through the dirty window panes. He saw Johnny's unblemished face as he leaned over the arm of the chair and peered through the window. In the sunlight, his hair was still sandy-yellow, almost golden. He knew that Johnny was watching the young blond girl walk past her house next door.

"You have not changed a bit, have you? Still have only one thing on your mind.

Stop looking at her like that. She's too young for you . . . . and too good for you, too.

My God! You must be forty years old now! Sure, you are the same age as my daughter. You should see my grandsons. They're my . . . .". He sat up again to have a better look at Johnny. "Come closer. I want to see you. You don't look a day older. How can that be, when the sands of time have taken such a toll on me?" For a moment the sands slowed to only a sprinkle, as his mind grabbed at a straw in the reverie which carried him back upstream to a time when life was good, when the days were all sunny and the nights deserved to be called "memorable", when they dared to surface in the stream of consciousness. But then the slow, steady flow of sand began again.

"No." He said, as he lay back on the pillow. "You have not changed even a little bit. I'll bet you still don't have a job, either. Well, you'll probably never need one. There will always be others."

The rays of sunshine had gone. He did not have to open his eyes to see that it was dark. He just knew. Still, he could not know if it was the same day or another day, or was it even day at all? Perhaps it was night. Maybe he had slept. It always seemed dark when the sand fell at a faster pace. Faster and faster with each hour, and with each day it became more difficult to brush it away. He remembered the waves of white sand in the Sahara. But it was still and silent even when there was a swish of wind across the dunes.

"I used to think maybe you would call me sometime, or that maybe one day you would just come in. Like now." He looked over toward the chair. "Are you here now?

Are you still here?" It did not matter. The sand was flowing too fast, too heavily too overwhelmingly for it to matter.

When he awoke, or became aware that he was awake, he was not sure if it was the same, or another day. If he could just push upward, rise above the mounting sand, life could be good again. Even if he could not be young again, still there could be good days and good times, and time to make more good memories. Even if there could not be love again, still there could be sunny days with flowers and birds. There could be cool raindrops and warm summer breezes once more if the sand would just become still like in the desert. But they had told him that it was not always still, that it is always changing, shifting with strong winds. Everything changes.

"Except for you, everything changes. You are exactly as you were when we were in London, and Paris and Brussels. Oh, no. That was someone else. You did not go with me."

For a few minutes the sand stopped as they walked beneath the towering chestnut trees in a park in Paris. Then suddenly he was sitting with his daughter on a park bench in London. But that was before Paris. And Brussels was later. Something was wrong. Nothing was in its chronological order, nothing in its right place. Time was mingled into a crumpled piece of blank paper wadded up and thrown into a trash heap of pleasure and disappointment. And the hot sand slowly covered his fevered body. He tried to pull himself above the sands. Breathing was difficult though the stream of falling sand was small, and slow to fall onto his fevered brow and stick to the drops of cold sweat which seemed to puddle there.

"Did you miss me? I often wondered if you ever thought about me. The good times. They were good, weren't they? It's hard to remember, hard to tell, because of the heartaches in between."

Another day of lightness and darkness, or perhaps it was two or three . . . . pass with the sand. In vain, he tries to lift himself above it. Now the sand falls with such force that it stings his eyes, his nose, his lips, and it makes his body shiver with fever. Like March winds that sweep the tiny grains off the Gobi desert and across Beijing, China, the sand drifts through the hourglass and stings his body while his spirit lies buried beneath his fevered skin, beneath the sand.

"Did you miss me when I was in Beijing? Did you even know that I went there?" He remembered beautiful Asian eyes, dimples, and hair as dark as night and as shiny as a sunny day. Jian and Xiaohong: the thought of them caused him to struggle with greater strength in his efforts to climb to the top of The Great Wall. Only it was a wall of sand now that pulled him down: the sands of time.

"You know I wanted it to be different. I wanted you to stay, but I knew you couldn't. I knew that I could not let you stay. I just want to know why you are here now, still so young, so beautiful."

When he opened his eyes again, it was mid-day, and the sun was shining. It was New Year's Eve, but in the South, it is often warm in early January. A new year. It would be a good year, 2007. On his bedside table lay the hourglass. Yes, he had broken it long ago and swept away the sand. He had broken it deliberately, in order to pour out the sand, because no longer was it fun to watch it fall through the hourglass. The broken pieces sparkled in the sunlight. He felt weak, but his fever was gone. The young man was gone, too. What did it matter? Springtime would come soon and all the world would be young and new again. He walked slowly to the kitchen and made a cup of hot tea.

Burying Alice Anne

By
Robert Bertrand

BURRYING ALICE ANNE

Could be a comedy or a tragedy, whatever the mood. In an early 1900's house somewhere in the South, live two aged, unwed sisters, Estelle and Agnes. The wall paper in the rather spacious parlor is faded and the furnishings could be antique or just old and shabby. Upstage center is a door leading to the hallway. From there, right is the front entrance, to the left is the back of the house and the bedrooms. Stage right has a window and stage left a door which leads to the dining room. Center stage has a couch, in front of which is a marble-top table.

To the left is a large chair near the dining room door. Upstage near the center door is a desk with drawers. Near the window on the right is an etegere. Down stage and off to the right is an open fireplace with a mantle with several collected objects. On the left side of the mantle there is an open space which has belonged to Alice Anne. The back of the fireplace is open in order not to block the audience's view. Beside the fireplace is a box for fire logs, which can be seen in the box. Agnes, the older sister, is straightening mother's picture to the right of the center stage door.

ESTELLE
(Coming in from hallway door, she is holding an armful of rages and a doll's head. She is historical.) Oh my God! Oh my God! Oh my God!

AGNES
Great God of Mercy, Estelle, what's wrong? (Seeing the rags in Estelle's arms) What in heaven's name is that?

ESTELLE

It's Alice Anne, you fool!

AGNES

(looking closer, curiously) It doesn't look like Alice Anne Oh my God! It's Alice Anne! What's happened to her? (She grabs part of the rags . . . . each sister stands looking at the rags they hold.) Estelle, what did you do to Alice Anne?

ESTELLE

I didn't do anything to her. (a beat) It was you, Agnes! You're the one who was taking her for a walk in the garden. You left her lying on the front porch swing.

AGNES

Well, maybe I did leave her out, but I certainly didn't chew her to shreads like this. I guess the neighbor's mean dog ripped her apart. She looks like the contents of a rag bag . . . . (Here, Agnes begins to "drift off" as she often does lately) or a quilt scrap box or a rat bed or a rag mop or . . .

ESTELLE

Woman, SHUT UP! (Estelle begins to cry) She's gone! Alice Anne is dead! Oh my God, she's DEAD!

AGNES

(is very calm now, almost noncaring) I'm afraid so.

ESTELLE

Murderer!

AGNES

(Turning away and back to her "straightening up things".) Oh, stop it Estelle. It's just a doll.

ESTELLE

(She moves to sit on sofa) It's your fault. You killed her. (She is crying again) Oh, oh, Alice Anne!

AGNES

(Sympathetic, almost apologetic) Essie, Essie, Essie, I'm so sorry this has happened to Alice Anne. But, after all, she wasn't your's. Alice Anne belonged to me. I didn't mean to forget her and leave her all alone on the front veranda, but you know how forgetful I've become these days.

ESTELLE

I know you didn't do it on purpose, sister, (still crying) But you know how much I loved her. She has been like a big sister to me. I wish you had remembered to bring her back inside (she moves over the mantel to the empty space) to her place here on the mantel.

AGNES

Seems like I just forget everything these days. I forget the laundry is in the dryer. (She is "off" again) I forget that the tea kettle is on forget birthdays . . . . people's names what day it is . . .

ESTELLE

Agnes! SHUT UP! (A beat) Oh, I'm sorry I'm yelling, sister, I know you tend to forget somethings . . . . EVERYTHING! (She cries) I'm just so upset over what's happened to Alice Anne.

(She calms herself and speaks softly, remembering) She's been with us for longer than seventy years, and now . . . she's gone. We'll miss her dreadfully. How can we live without her? She always sat there on the fireplace mantle. It's so sad. It's a terrible, terrible thing to happen She moves stage left)

AGNES

(Almost to the audience as much as to Estelle) Well, after all . . . . she was only a doll

ESTELLE

ONLY A DOLL? Agnes Murcheson, how can you say she was only a doll? She was like our sister. She was like my big sister.

AGNES

(Pondering) I thought that I was your big sister. Yes, yes, I do remember that much, Essie.

ESTELLE

Well, you know how much I loved ALICE ANNE.

AGNES

You mean that you love her more than you love me, Essie? (With great concern) Does that mean you don't love me?

ESTELLE

No, I don't mean that . . . . but Alice Anne was always there for me . . . . when I was little, even when I was a bad girl, she was always there for me.

AGNES

Where was I, Essie?

ESTELLE

You were never there. I mean well, I don't know where you were! (She now moves over to the mantel again, and places the pile of rags and the doll head on the space reserved for Alice Anne) Oh, Alice Anne. It will never be the same. (She moves on to gaze out the window)

AGNES

(She has followed Estelle and heaps her pile of rags upon the others. She pats them up into a neat little pile. She is facing the audience) Where was I, Estelle?

ESTELLE

(Turning to face her sister) What?

AGNES

You said I was never there for you. Where was I?

ESTELLE

Well, you were there . . . . but you never played with me like Alice Anne did.

AGNES

How can you say that. Of course I played with you. I know I'm forgetful, but I do remember playing with you. I remember all the fun we had. I shared everything with you. I shared my toys with you . . . . (She's off) I shared my clothes . . . . my books . . . . my make-up . . . . my pretty new umbrella . . . .

ESTELLE

Oh, stop it, Agnes.

AGNES

My BOYFRIEND!

ESTELLE

What?

AGNES

My boyfriend, Estelle! I shared my boyfriend with you. (She faces her sister eye to eye) No! I didn't share him with you YOU TOOK HIM . . . . you took him away from me.

ESTELLE

I didn't know that you ever knew about that.

AGNES

Of course I knew. Why else would I have broken my engagement to him? I loved him. I planned to be his wife. But I found out about you and him . . . . I found out what you did together. I couldn't marry him then.

ESTELLE

All those years . . . . and you never said anything to me about it, until now.

AGNES

I never said anything to you and I never said anything to him. But he knew. He knew why I gave his ring back.

ESTELLE

I'm sorry. (There is nothing else she can say)

AGNES

You took my future husband to bed with you. And you took Alice Anne away from me just like you took him.

ESTELLE

What does that mean?

AGNES

Alice Anne was mine. (Over to mother's picture) Mother gave her to me on my first birthday. Then, when you came along, she made me let her sleep with you . . . . and I had to sleep alone.

ESTELLE

She was here for both of us.

AGNES

Every time I took her away from you, you cried. Mother would make me give her back to you. You took everything that was mine! You took my clothes . . . .

ESTELLE

They were hand-me-downs that you had outgrown. You always got the new stuff.

AGNES

Only to have you take them away from me! You always got what you wanted. You took everything you wanted that was mine, including the man I planned to spend the rest of life with. So, I never got to leave home. I had to spend the rest of life here with you!

ESTELLE

I couldn't help being born a cripple. I can't help if no man found me attractive. Paul was the only chance I ever had to have a man. He was caring and gentle and he lift me to the front porch swing during those times when I couldn't walk. Then he would lift me back to my bed upstairs. It just happened . . . IT JUST HAPPENED! I didn't plan for it to happen (calmer) How did you find out about it?

AGNES

(Still looking at mother's picture) In spite of mother's great effort to keep anyone from finding out, I knew that you miscarried the baby. I knew that Paul was the only man who had that kind of opportunity with you.

ESTELLE

He loved you. You should have married him anyway.

AGNES

Not after what you did. I knew that you would have to depend on me after mother and papa were gone, and I couldn't stand the thought of Paul and you and me living together. (Her mood changes) But that's all in the past. I have things to do. (She turns away)

ESTELLE

Oh, oh . . . . (She begins to cry again) Oh, my, oh, me.

AGNES

Stop crying, Essie. I said it's in the past.

ESTELLE

I'm crying about Alice Anne!

AGNES

Good Lord, Essie, it's just a doll. Now leave me alone. I have to make the funeral arrangements.

SCENE II

There is a cardboard box on the marble-top table in front of the couch. The box, decorated with ribbons and flowers, is covered with a lid that is secured with duct tape. Agnes enters from stage left. Estelle follows.

ESTELLE

Sister, you didn't eat your dinner. You didn't even touch your tapioca.

AGNES

You know I don't like tapioca and I hate fried chicken . . . . (She's off) . . . and roast and corn and okra and tomatoes . . . . and succotash . . . and . . .

ESTELLE

Agnes . . . . (bored with it) come back!

AGNES

(She does) Where was I? Oh, yes, we have to burry Alice Anne. I fixed her coffin before I went to bed last night. (She picks up the box, lovingly) We'll lay her to rest in the garden in the back yard.

ESTELLE

Yes, under the crepe myrtle tree. I'll fetch a spade from the storage room.

SCENE III

The sisters return. Estelle is holding a spade. She has been crying again.

AGNES

Well, it's all over.

ESTELLE

It will never be over, Sister. I will always miss Alice Anne.

AGNES

I will miss her, too. And I miss mother and papa, too. And I miss the circus . . . . and the dances the hummingbirds the hayrides . . .

ESTELLE

Agnes! You never went on a hayride in your life!

AGNES

And I miss PAUL. I miss Paul every day of my life. You had no right to him. He was mine. I had my wedding dress bought. It hangs in my closet still never worn! (She is about to collapse, a used, sad old lady) You had no right to him He had no right to you . . . You were my sister . . . He betrayed me, and Alice Anne betrayed me . . . she always preferred you . . . YOU, YOU, YOU! You always ruined everything!

(Cruel) Not everything, Agnes. It was you who was responsible for the dogs destroying Alice Anne!

AGNES

The dogs didn't kill her! I did! I did it. It was ME. I took the garden clippers and I cut her to shreads!

ESTELLE

(Stunned) Why? Never mind, why! I don't even want to know why. I have stayed here with you only because you need a keeper, you need someone to take care of you . . . . You're too forgetful to stay by yourself. You need help . . . but not from me. I can't stay with you anymore.

AGNES

GO! I don't care . . . I want you to go. I don't need you . . . I don't need Paul, and I don't need Alice Anne. She didn't care for me anyway. I cut her up because she loved you best. She always loved you, not me. (She turns to the picture of mother on the wall) DIDN'T SHE, MOTHER?

ESTELLE

Agnes, she was only a doll. I'll pack my things tonight. I'll leave tomorrow morning.

SCENE IV

No one is in the parlor. On the table in front of the couch is the box the sisters buried the day before. It has been opened. The ribbons and flowers dangle loosely, and the tape hangs in front of the marble top table. Agnes enters from the kitchen. She does not notice the box. Estelle enters from hallway. Agnes sees her and makes a point of turning away from her. In so doing, she sees the box.

AGNES

Oh my God! It's Alice Anne's coffin. You DUG HER UP?

ESTELLE

(She has reached the table. She removes the lid from the box . . . and pulls out a log . . . . one that was in the box beside the fireplace. Holding up the log . . .) A LOG, Agnes! A damn fire log. You buried a fire log instead of Alice Anne.

AGNES

You had no right to exhume that coffin! Pilfering with a grave is against the law!

ESTELLE

You're a crazy old fool, Agnes. CRAZY. Where is she? What did you do with her?

AGNES

(She hurries over to the desk and stands guard over it.) I'll not tell you where she is. You can't make me!

ESTELLE

Oh, Agnes, you can't fool me. I know where she is she's behind the chair! (Estelle starts toward the chair. Agnes runs ahead of her. Estelle then runs to the desk and pulls a drawer open and takes out the dolls head.

AGNES

No . . . No! She's mine! She's mine . . . . and Paul is mine and . . . (she drifts off) . . . and . . . What was I saying? Who are you? Where am I? Mother! Mother! Where am I? Where are we?

ESTELLE

(She goes to her sister and places the doll head in her hand) You take her, sister. She belongs to you.

AGNES

(Clutching the dolls head to her breast) Where am I? Oh my God, I don't know where I am. I don't remember my name . . . . What's happening to me?

ESTELLE

Come on, Sister. I'll help you to your bed. You'll feel better after you have some rest. (They exit center stage door together.)

SCENE V

The two sisters are in the parlor. Estelle is sitting on the couch with a sewing basket, possibly working on a quilt top. Agnes is arranging things on the etegere. Then she moves over to the mantle and begins to arrange things which are on the mantle, spacing them about to take up the empty space where Alice Anne used to sit.

AGNES

I just thought that I might restore Alice Anne to health. That's why I hid her remains in the desk drawer and burned a fire log instead. I thought maybe I could stuff her little insides back inside., sew her up again, tie her little cracked head back on . . . her little feet . . . her hands . . . . her

ESTELLE

Agnes, it was hopeless. She's gone . . . . to wherever all . . . . good dolls go. At least she's buried along with all our problems. Remember, we've buried with Alice Anne, anything that would cause us to worry. Just try to remember that.

AGNES

I will try to remember. But you will have to help me. You know I tend to forget things like birthdays names . . . .

ESTELLE

Yes, how well I know. And I am going to be here to help you. But I'm going to help you remember only the happy times.

AGNES

Yes! And there were some happy times, weren't there?

ESTELLE

Many, and what's more, there are going to be lots of happy times yet.

AGNES

I'm tired now, Essie. I think I'll go to bed and get some rest. Good night. (She walks to hallway door, turns) Essie, I'm glad you didn't leave me here alone.

ESTELLE

(She smiles as her sister leaves center door. Then she gets up from couch cautiously, steals over to the large chair, and pulls from behind it, Alice Anne's coffin. She takes it to the couch, places it on the table in front of her and takes Alice Anne's head, scraps and all out of the box. After seconds of wondering where to begin, she is stitching Alice Anne together again.)

JEANS

A story of high-school friendships

BY
ROBERT BERTRAND

PROLOGUE

If you can deal well with disappointment, perhaps even in some constructive way, then set your goals high, be daring and adventuresome, but ever mindful that the more you expect from life, the more disappointments with which you will have to live.

Two years out of high school and even the best of friends begin to wonder why they were ever friends at all. For those who are brave enough, or curious enough, to attend the ten-year reunion, it is like culture shock, and you wonder who these strange people wearing false faces are, and how they could possibly have fit into your life at some time in the past.

For each classmate, individual experiences during twelve school years are as different as the lives they happen to stumble into afterward.

It is often said that life is what you make of it. That is only partially true. Life is what you make of it from circumstances that flirt with you and lead you down a path you never even saw before you. Or, it's what you can make of it in spite of circumstances that, without warning, jump up and slap you in the face . . . every time you crawl back up on your knees and try again.

"You can make it, if you only believe in yourself!" Questionable encouragement. Always, however, be alert to the unspecified number of opportunities that the world has to offer you.

JEANS

(At recess, on the bleachers)

GREG

I'm going to miss it. But I'll be happy when we're finished.

MARK

What's to miss? Too much homework, teachers who deliberately try to provoke you, morons for classmates . . . . mean coaches . . . . SOS in the lunchroom.

ROBBY

Mark, you are always so negative about school. My teachers have been great to me. Most of them, any way. Our fellow students are nice enough, so long as we don't try to hang out with them. The cafeteria food is . . . . well, it's cafeteria food. And you don't do your homework any way. And your best friends are Greg and I. So, you have nothing to complain about.

GREG

I'm sure you'll miss something about high school, Mark.

MARK

You guys. That's all. I can't think of anything else. What will you miss about it?

GREG

Besides you guys, I'll miss football mostly. But I'll miss the dances, too. I'll miss flirting with the girls. Our friends, our talks in the hallway . . . . everything! Especially Mrs. Adams.

ROBBY

Well, maybe Mark has a point. You do have more to miss than we do. You're on the team, you're popular with the guys, you got girlfriends, you're 'teacher's pet', especially Mrs. Adams'. Mark and I are not in your league. I'm surprised that you hang out with us. If we didn't live on the same street, you probably wouldn't.

GREG

You'd still be my friends regardless of where we live.

MARK

Yeah, right! You'd ignore us just like all the others do.

ROBBY

Yeah. But I'll miss it all, too. But what I'll miss the most is the individual attention we get here. In college, you know, it's going to be different. We won't get the individual attention we get here from our teachers. We'll either sink or swim, and the instructor won't even remember your name.

MARK

I won't be in college. Out on my own is where I want to be. That's where I will be. I'll have a life of my own, to do what I want to do anytime I want to do it . . . . whatever it is that I want to do.

ROBBY

What do you mean, you won't be in college. We've talked about college before. You have to go to college. There're no jobs here. The way life is today, you can't even get a decent job without a college degree. Sure, you're going to college.

MARK

I'm just looking forward to going *away.* Forget college.

GREG

I wish we could all go off together. Man, wouldn't that be great to be in college together?

MARK

What would be so great about that? The campus is so big; we'd never see each other. You'd be hanging out with the sports guys. Robby would be king of the nerds. I'd be . . . . nobody, just like here in high school.

ROBBY

We could never be on the same campus, any way. You'll probably get a football scholarship to the university. I have to go to Birmingham Southern. That's my parents decision, and they are paying for it.

GREG

Yeah. You're right. I want to play for The University of Alabama. It will be great if I can go there.

MARK

It will be great if I can just *go*! Anywhere. Except to college. I just want to go and get the hell out of Dodge.

GREG

Mark, I'm telling you, man, you've got to go to college. You should go to the University of Alabama with me. I know you can work it out if you just try!

MARK

What makes you think so? Nothing else I've tried ever worked out. Besides, my grades are too low. My parents won't support me.

And . . . . *I* just plain hate school and studying . . . . and all the rest of the shit that goes with it.

GREG

It will be different in college, man. There must be something you like about school, even if it is not studying. Something?

MARK

Well, let's see. Nope, so far . . . . ***nothing!***

ROBBY

Nothing. After twelve years? Well, we have a few more months before we graduate. Maybe you will experience something that will entice you to apply for college before graduation.

(In the hallway, at lockers)

MARK

An "F"! A fucking "F". I'm going to fucking fail chemistry! I'm not going to fucking graduate! My dad is going to fucking kill me!

GREG

He should kill you. Mark, you're intelligent enough to pass chemistry. Besides, Robby told you that he'd help you. He makes "A's" in everything . . . . and he's offered to tutor you many times.

MARK

You don't have to remind me. I know he makes "A's" in everything, and he never lets anybody forget it, especially me.

GREG

Well, he's a good student, and he works hard for his grades. His parents already have the money saved up for his college expenses. They're very proud of him. I am, too! And you should be, too. He doesn't brag about his grades, he only offers to help you.

MARK

Yeah. I know. I'm happy for him, too. I'm sure he just wants to help me. But I don't want his help, because I'm not going to college . . . . much to my parents' dismay. But they aren't dismayed enough to say they will pay for it. I'd have to borrow money to go. Anyway, if I don't get my grades up, I won't even graduate from high school.

GREG

Robby and I won't let you fail. We're all going off to college, even if not to the same one. Stop thinking negatively about it, and just study harder, so you can get into at least a community college. I'm trying not to think of the possibility that I might not get a scholarship. Because if I don't, I won't be able to go to The University of Alabama and play football. That's always been my dream.

MARK

You'll get it. You're the best.

GREG

Maybe the best here, at Greenwood High, but I'll be up against guys from all over the country, all of them wanting the same thing I do. And if I don't get that scholarship, I may not get to go. My folks cannot afford to pay.

MARK

My dad can afford to pay for me to go, but he won't. He's has already said that my college experience would be a bad investment for him, because I'm so fucking stupid . . . . lazy . . . . too much like . . . .

GREG

It's a good thing that you have that fast-food job. You can always flip burgers for the rest of your life.

MARK

Right! Screw that! As soon as I graduate, if I graduate, I'm out of here!

GREG

There's the bell. Recess is over. I've got computer class. See you.

MARK

Right. I've got art with queery O'leary. Hey, set me up with your computer teacher, Miss Hammonds. Tell her I'm in the prime of my life and she's wasting all my good prime by not going out with me.

GREG

Man, you know she's married! Besides that, she's thirty something and wouldn't waste her time on a weeny penis like you.

MARK

She's the hottest thing on campus! And don't compare my dick with a weeny! You're not that much bigger than me. I'll be ready to take another measurement and compare with you anytime!

GREG

When you see Robby, tell him to meet us after football practice. It's "jack-off contest time again!

(in study hall I library)

GREG

I never said we **did it**. Even if we had, I wouldn't tell you guys. After all, she might be the one. I might just marry her someday. And if I do, what we do on our dates is not something I would want to share with you.

MARK

Come on, man. She's just another cunt. No different than the others you've had. We just want to know what it's like. I think I'm accurate in saying that Robby hasn't had it yet, no more than I have.

ROBBY

We know you've done her. You get all your dates. You might as well confess. Give us a thrill. Vicariously is the only way we'll ever get it.

GREG

I didn't say that I didn't. I just said that I don't want to talk about it, not about **her**, because she's different. Just shut up about it, OK?

MARK

Man, you're lucky! How many does this make? Six? Eight?

GREG

I don't **count** them. Sixteen! But like I said, who's counting? (they laugh)

TEACHER

Quiet, boys! Mark, this is why you are failing chemistry. You never apply yourself, nor use your time wisely.

GREG

(whispered) And you never think about anything except sex. (laugh, unnoticed)

MARK

You got that right. That's all I want to do . . . . sex, I mean, and the sad thing is that I am probably the only Senior who doesn't get any. We're only young once. A few more years and youth's sweet song will turn into a funeral hymn at least as far as getting it up is concerned.

GREG

No way, man, we were born at just the right time. We're lucky to be young now . . . at this point in time. Women have sexual freedom they want to do it as much as we do. And they say that our generation could live to be over a hundred. Just think, with the invention of Viagra, Levitra, Cialis all that kind of stuff, we could still be doing it when we're in our nineties.

ROBBY

Yeah, but just think what we'll be screwing; ninety-year old ladies.

GREG

Older men can always get younger women.

MARK

That's what I want now. An older woman, like Miss Hammonds. My brother dates older women. He says they like younger men because they think they can train them to do what they like. He says they know how to please a guy, because they have more experience. But I think he dates older women because they take care of him when he's out of a job . . . . and he usually is, most of the time. He left home when he was sixteen. He told me once that he left home because he could never please our dad. I think he was right.

ROBBY

Are you going to let me help you with your chemistry assignment, or are you going to talk about women?

MARK

Chemistry is not as important as . . . . ***nothing*** is more important than getting laid! Especially if you've never been laid. And *you* should know that as well as I do, Robby. I get hard just thinking about it.

GREG

Me, too. I'm going to jack-off as soon as I get home.

MARK

Hey, man, let's have one of our contests. Your parents won't be home until five.

ROBBY

I think I should go home and study. My parents got on to me the last time I was late.

MARK

As horny as I am, it will only take a few minutes. Come on, guys! Let's do it.

GREG

Have your five bucks ready. First one off gets the pot.

ROBBY

OK. I'm in.

(Shooting hoops, Robby's)

ROBBY

He's new. I met him in the library yesterday. He should have been here by now. I guess he's not coming.

MARK

What's he like?

ROBBY

What do you mean? Like, is he tall, short, black, white, smart like me, stupid like you?

MARK

No, I mean is he a cute little prick like you that we all want to fuck! I just asked a simple question. Forget about it.

ROBBY

Well, if you wanted to know if he's good-looking like me, why didn't you just ask.

GREG

What difference does it make? Who cares what he looks like, so long as he can shoot hoops, and play cards with us, or likes fishing. So long as he's not a crack-head, nor does a lot of drinking. What about sports? Does he like sports?

ROBBY

I guess. He's coming to shoot with us. Maybe. He should have been here before now.

GREG

What about football? Is he going to be on the team?

ROBBY

Don't worry. Even if he is, he won't give you any competition for that scholarship. He's not as big as you are. Doesn't look very strong. I don't know that much about him. We didn't talk about sports.

MARK

Well, what did you talk about, ass hole?

ROBBY

I don't know . . . . classes, teachers, families, you guys.

MARK

What? What about *us?*

ROBBY

I told him you are two of the biggest nut cases I ever met. Just wait until you meet him, then you can ask him everything you want to know about him.

GREG

Did he tell you where he came from? Never mind. I'll ask him myself. Let's change the subject. I've got football practice tomorrow after school.

MARK

What are you guys doing after the game Friday night?

GREG

I've got a date. Karen.

ROBBY

I'm still looking for a birthday present for Lukeysha. One that just lets her know I'm noticing her, but not one that makes her think I really like her, in case she does not like me, and she probably doesn't. My parents are taking me to the mall.

MARK

My parents are going out of town. I have to go with them. It's my grandma's birthday.

GREG

What kind of a name is Lukeysha? Who is she? You haven't even mentioned her before. Why don't you take her out? That's not making a commitment to anything. Just ask her for a date.

ROBBY

I do want to get to know her, but I don't want to put myself in a position to be rejected. Besides, once we get to know each other, if we get that far, she probably won't even like me. I might not even like her. I just like the way she looks and the way she acts around other students.

GREG

Take her on a date and get to know her. That's the best way. But you can't wait until she asks you.

MARK

And if you don't date her, how you gonna fuck her?

ROBBY

Shut up, Mark! That's all you ever think about . . . . Hey, here he comes. Hey, Giovanni, we thought you weren't going to show.

GIOVANNI

I had to help my dad do a few things before I could get away. I'm sorry I'm late. Are you still shooting?

ROBBY

Yeah. This is Greg, Mark. Guys, this is Giovanni.

GREG

Hey, Giovanni, 's'up?

MARK

Hey, man, you like pussy?

ROBBY

Just get used to him, Giovanni. He's girl crazy . . . . sex crazy . . . . or just plain crazy! Ignore him.

GREG

When I'm not having football practice, we shoot hoops. We need you. Mark and me against Robby and you. Let's do it! (he puts it through)

GIOVANNI

I thought football was over.

MARK

It's never over for him. Our team is in the playoffs, thanks to Greg. Besides, he practices year round. Trying to get a scholarship for college. What's your sport? I'm not good at any . . . . except swimming. I'm a good swimmer. We don't have a swimming team at school. Don't even have a pool.

ROBBY

We swim in the heated pool at the "Y". Except in the summer, we go to the creek and go skinny dipping.

GIOVANNI

That's great. I'll go with you sometime. I'm a good swimmer. I could have been great, but my mom well, taking me to the pool to practice was not her favorite thing to do. Yeah, I like swimming. The skinny part . . . . I don't know, never did that before.

GREG

You ever go fishing? We like to go over to my dad's lake to fish. We can swim there, too.

GIOVANNI

I've never been fishing before. But I'd like to try it.

GREG

I'll fix you up a pole.

MARK

Speaking of poles, Greg's is . . .

GREG

Shut up, Mark! We watch movies at my place sometimes. We have a basement and I have a TV in it.

MARK

Yeah, and sometimes I can get my hands on some of my dad's hot flicks, if you know what I mean.

GIOVANNI

Great! I like "hot flicks" and, yes, I like pussy, too.

(Walking on Sidewalk)

GIOVANNI

It's too cold to shoot hoops. Let's go for a swim at the "Y".

MARK

Yeah. That's a good idea. I was there yesterday after school. The water was just right.

GIOVANNI

It's great to have a heated pool so near. I didn't have one close by when I lived in Florida, and, like I told you, my mom wouldn't drive me across town. She always had other things to do. And my sister still didn't have her driver's license then. By the way, my sister is visiting my dad and me this week-end. Who's going to volunteer to date her?

MARK

If she's as good looking as you . . . . I mean, you know . . . cute, I'll date her.

GREG

I'm going steady, kind of. Anyway, Karen thinks we are. But I'll date her, if I don't have to promise not to do her.

GIOVANNI

You wouldn't be her first! But if you do, just don't tell me about it. **She** will tell me more than I want to know! She's bringing two of her friends with her. I'm dating one of them. So, I guess you get the third one, Mark.

MARK

Oh! I just remembered that I have to baby-sit with my little cousin. Sorry. Robby, I think you will have to be her date.

ROBBY

Sure. I'm in. We can go to a movie and then party at my house later. My parents will be gone out of town over the week-end.

MARK

Good. Well, that's settled. Now let's get our bathing suits and towels.

(At the Pool)

GIOVANNI

(In the showers, after swimming) That was great. I'm really happy to have a pool so near where we live.

ROBBY

Say, Greg, what if Karen finds out about you dating Giovanni's sister.

GREG

Well, it's like I said, we're not really going steady. I'm just not really into her that much. And she doesn't like sucking well, you know, doing that. Besides, the coach has told me to save my strength and to not get into girls all that much. He says that it could ruin my chances for that scholarship, if I spend too much time screwing around.

MARK

So, you let coach control your sex life? If Karen doesn't like doing it, then you should find someone who does. Or maybe you're just too big for her to take it! You brag about how big you are all the time.

GREG

I do not! I could though. I'm definitely bigger than you! I still remember the "jack-off contests we used to have when we were in junior high school. You hadn't even gone through puberty.

MARK

Yes, I had!

GREG

Oh. Well, it just didn't look like you had!

MARK

Screw you, Greg! OK, so I was a late bloomer. The important thing is that I think I can measure up to your size now! Want proof? Let's have another contest.

GIOVANNI

What the hell is a "Jack-off contest? You guys are weird!

ROBBY

We used to go down to the creek, or down in Greg's basement and we would all put five bucks in the pot. The one who gets off the quickest, wins the pot.

GREG

I think it's time for Mr. Big-mouth Mark to show us all this new growth he's had since junior high school.

MARK

I'll do just that, Mr. Show-off! And I think it's time for Giovanni to show us what he's got. He won't even go to the bathroom during recess, when the other guys are in there.

GREG

Yeah. How about it, Giovanni? Tomorrow night in my basement. Are you in, or are you afraid I'll put you to shame?

GIOVANNI

I can't believe I'm saying this, but, yes, I'm in. I'm timid about . . . . being seen, but I think I can measure up to any of you. I've never pulled it out in front of anyone, not even my dad. But you guys are weird! If you get too weird, I'm out. I mean, I can't be your friend. And I don't have any other friends, so don't invite me into some mixed up mess. OK?

ROBBY

Trust me, Giovanni. It's just a fun thing. We're going back a few years to our younger days, when we were just as shy about it as you are.

MARK

But there is just one change in the contest. It's not who gets off the quickest, it is who has the biggest dick that wins the pot. Besides, I've learned that it is not good to get off too quick. It's called "pre-mature ejaculation". And women don't like that.

GREG

You must have been reading some sex books. I know you have not even done it with a girl, so you must have been reading-up on how to do it right.

(After the Movie at Robby's House)
(Robby and Annette)

ROBBY

What? You don't like Black boys?

ANNETTE

Don't even go there! I have nothing against Black boys that I don't have against *all* boys. You're all jerks! You never want to do anything but . . . that! That's all you ever think about.

ROBBY

No. You're wrong! I study a lot. I have many different interests. Maybe I do think about it a lot, but that doesn't mean I'm always trying to do it with someone. In fact, I never have!

ANNETTE

Oh, my God! You mean you're a virgin? You're a Senior in high school and you're still a . . .

ROBBY

Yes! Yes, I'm still I've never had a girl. I just hoped that tonight, with you . . . . I wanted to do it before graduation.

ANNETTE

Just so that you can say you did it. Well, I have done it, and take my word for it, it is not that great! There is more to life than that, and I think that you are one who knows that. Maybe you're the only male in the world that knows that there are better things in life than . . . . that, but I believe you do.

ROBBY

I thought you came here on this date for that purpose.

ANNETTE

To have sex with you? No! It's not often a girl gets to date a really intelligent boy. Can't we just talk about something important? Like, maybe Leo De Caprio's new movie?

ROBBY

God! You should have dated Mark. He would have talked all night about him. You would think he has the hots for Leo.

(Giovanni and Elaine)

GIOVANNI

It doesn't matter to me that you're a virgin really, I don't mind. I want to do it anyway! Hell, I'm a virgin, too. Come on, let me have it . . . . please . . . just let me feel of it at least!

ELAINE

No! I told you, I'm saving myself for the right guy, for the one I'm going to marry someday.

GIOVANNI

I'll never tell him, I promise! Come on, let's do it.

ELAINE

You are so crude! Stop doing that! No, I don't want you to do that. You're a jerk!

GIOVANNI

Well, maybe, but that doesn't stop me from being horny! Just feel how hard I am, Elaine, baby, sweetheart!

ELAINE

Oh! It is hard, and **big!** But I told you that I'm saving myself for that special man I'm looking for.

GIOVANNI

Well, you just found him! If what you're holding in your hand doesn't make me a special man Oh, oh! I'll love you, I'll marry you . . . . I . . . I. Oh!

ELAINE

Shit! Why did you go and do that? It's all in my hand . . . and on my new dress!

(Greg and Maria)

GREG

But you didn't ask. And besides, it doesn't matter, because officially she's not my steady girlfriend.

MARIA

You shouldn't be dating me if you already have a girlfriend. I'm not the type of girl who moves in on another girl's territory. Take your hand away from there. Go feel on your girlfriend.

GREG

I told you, she's not really my girlfriend. But forget about it. I was just doing your brother a favor by dating you anyway.

MARIA

You want to do my brother a favor? Then go fuck him!

GREG

Whatever. I'm going home. Nice meeting you, Maria.

MARIA

I don't think so! Now you've got me all hot and wet, you're not going anywhere until you satisfy me. If you date me, you lay me! That's my motto! Don't touch that zipper. I'll unzip you myself. That's the only foreplay I need.

(In Greg's Car)

GREG

It's hard to believe it's happened. We've known him since first grade.

MARK

I never thought much about it, you know . . . . death. Why should we have to think about dying until we get old? Death is not for young people like us.

GREG

I'll bet George Johnson never thought too much about it either . . . . until his wreck last week-end. Man, that's gotta be tough for his parents. He died before the rescue squad could get him to the hospital. Guys, we will never drink before we drive.

ROBBY

That's not the only reason young people die. It could have been any number reasons.

GREG

But they say that that was *his* reason. Man, it really sucks! Just think how his parents must feel. Just think how we would feel if it was one of us, or all of us at the same time. Right now, I am just extra careful while I'm driving us around.

ROBBY

I think about death sometimes. I wonder what it's like. I wonder if it's scary. Seems like it would be, I know it is to me, not knowing where you go after . . . . being with strange people, or with no one.

GIOVANNI

Scared of what, just being with people you don't know?

ROBBY

I don't know. I guess it's just kind of scary thinking about it. Maybe after it's over there would be nothing to be scared of.

GREG

That's just it. You don't know. That's what's scary about it. They say the unknown is what is scary about everything . . . . or anything that is scary.

MARK

How can you be afraid of something you don't know? I don't think I'm afraid of anything. And who knows, maybe George is happier wherever he is than he was here. Ever think of that?

ROBBY

You know, Mark, sometimes you are kinda weird. And you must be afraid of something. Everyone is. You have to be afraid of something.

MARK

Nope. I can't think of a single thing that I'm afraid of. I guess if there was something I am afraid of, it would be my dad.

GIOVANNI

What about snakes, and wasps, and what about wild animals like bears and lions? What about queers? What about old people? I was afraid of my grandmother.

MARK

That's stupid! Why are you afraid of an old lady?

GIOVANNI

Well, I'm not anymore, because she's dead now. But I used to be afraid that she would die while I was in the room with her. Alone with her.

MARK

Well, when she died, it was not like she was going to take everyone in the room with her. If she did, you must have run like hell, because you're still here. I know if my granny died and took everyone in the room with her, I'd sure haul ass, because there is no telling which direction she's going in.

GIOVANNI

Well, I think I know where my grandmother went. She was a good old lady, at least to me.

MARK

Oh, I know where mine is going when she dies. She's going straight to hell. Actually, I think she **came** from hell.

ROBBY

I'm not afraid of many things. If I am afraid of something, it would be people. I'm more comfortable with animals than I am people. I am especially afraid of people who don't like animals.

GREG

I'm afraid of dying and going to hell. I mean, I don't think I am, but I really want to start being more . . . well, better. You know, a better person, like going to church, praying, talking to Jesus . . . . stuff like that. I used to go to church with my parents when I was little. I want to start back.

MARK

You're as good as I am, and I go every Sunday, almost. It's all in what you want to do with it . . . with what you learn from it and put into practice, I mean.

GREG

What do you mean? "It's all in what you want to do with it." What?

MARK

Well, I mean . . . people say that we need to "accept" him. That we need to pray, that we need to "take" Him in our hearts. We need to thank Him . . . but I don't know how to do any of that stuff.

GIOVANNI

That's just what Greg was saying, that he needs to start back to going to church. That's how you learn all "that stuff. You have to go to church with the right attitude, you have to listen, and you have to make up you mind that you will make changes.

MARK

Like what? What kind of changes?

ROBBY

Like getting your mind on your lessons, and off sex so much of the time. Like when you are in the classroom, think about what is taking place in the classroom. And when you are in Sunday School, you should be listening to the teacher instead of day dreaming and going off into a fantasy, thinking of P-U-S-S-Y.

MARK

If God didn't want me to think about it, He wouldn't have invented it! And he wouldn't have made it something that I like thinking about. And my brother, the one that died, was a good student, and he went to church, but he died anyway!

GREG

You don't go to church to keep from dying, Mark. You go to church to help you understand how to not go to the bad place when you do die. And your life has nothing to do with what happened to your little brother.

GIOVANNI

Someday, I'm going to a church.

ROBBY

Giovanni, why are you afraid of snakes and . . . . queers?

GREG

Anybody want a hamburger? I'm hungry enough I could eat a snake!

MARK

(In the Library)

GREG

Man is she ever hot!

ROBBY

You know it, man! Would I ever like to spend a night with her!

GIOVANNI

A week-end would be better!

ROBBY

You couldn't handle that much heat all week-end!

GIOVANNI

And you could? I don't think so. I'll bet you a million bucks that I can get off more times than you can in a week-end.

ROBBY

No way. You get off too quick, anyway. She wouldn't even spend the first night with you. Women like for you to keep on pumping before you blow. I'll bet you would shoot your wad before you even get in her good.

GREG

Yeah. You or Mark one is always the first to blow, when we all do it together in my basement. It's getting warm enough now that we can go down to the creek, like we used to do. Mark would always be the first to finish, but now that you are here, speedy has some competition.

MARK

I may get off fast the first time, but I can do it again real quick. Before any of you can. The first time is for me, the second time is for her.

GREG

Her being Mrs. Palm and her five daughters. You didn't even get in that girl from Florida.

MARK

You don't know how many girls I've had, so just shut up! Anyway, I don't want to talk about it. I've got some issues with my dad.

ROBBY

What kind of issues, Mark?

MARK

Mainly, the issue that I hate the SOB. Or maybe it's just that he hates me. I don't know.

GREG

Well, let's go down to the creek and do something to get your mind off some of those issues. It's not too cold today.

GIOVANNI

I won't be going. I don't like watching you guys masturbate. It's just plain weird. I do it, too, but I don't like doing it while you guys watch.

GREG

Well, it seems like you've got issues, too. Maybe it turns you on to see guys naked.

MARK
Yeah! Does it, Giovanni? Does my dong excite you?

GIOVANNI
Now I **know** I'm not going. I don't even want to hear you talk about it, so just shut the fuck up.

GREG
Oh, come on, Giovanni. We're just teasing you. We know you like girls. But this afternoon at the creek, will be special, because we're going measure! I'm going to show all of you who's got the biggest dick. I'll prove I'm still the king!

MARK
Giovanni, you have to be there. We're going to measure you even if we have to hold you down, get you up and then measure you!

GIOVANNI
No fucking way, man. You guys are not going to touch my prick! . . . not with a ruler, not with your hand . . . . and not with your **mouth** if that's what you have in mind! You guys are freaking me out. That stuff is all you ever think about.

ROBBY
That's true about Mark for sure. He's probably got a hard on right now. He walks down the hallway with a hard on.

GREG
Go to the creak with us, Giovanni. I promise we won't take turns fucking your cute little ass.

TEACHER
Boys, you should be studying and not talking. If you continue to talk in study time, I'll have to separate you to different tables.

(Greg and Mark tossing football)

GREG
Who are you taking to the prom?

MARK
My parents are making me take my cousin, Louise. She's two or three years older than me. Since she never got asked to a prom, my mother says that I have to carry her. She's a real dog, but I'm stuck with her.

GREG
Too bad, no nookie for you . . . . unless she's a kissing cousin.

MARK
Well, I'm not. Besides, she's as ugly as a mud fence, which is why she was never asked to a prom when she was in school. I'm guessing that you're taking Karen.

GREG
No. I found out that she's been seeing someone else. I'm taking Maria, you know, Giovanni's sister. She's coming up from Florida just for the prom.

MARK
Oh, yeah? Well, I guess she really liked that big dick of yours.

GREG
I never dated one yet that didn't! And she's a really good fuck. She's pretty. She'll look real good at the prom. And after the prom, I'll make her really happy again.

MARK
As much as you aggravate me, Greg, I'll have to admit that I am really envious of you. You get all the girls, all you want, anyway, because you're the best looking guy in school. I get nothing,

something else that I hate to admit. The closest I ever got was when I was touched down there, not even stroked off. Actually, I just came as soon as . . . . my prick was touched.

GREG

Stop worrying about it, Mark. You'll have sex someday. Some kind of sex. It may not be exactly what you want, but you'll do something with someone someday. I remember my first time was different from what I thought it would be. I just try to forget about it. It will happen to you when you least expect it to, so there's no need to go looking for it from someone that really turns you on. It will find you.

MARK

I don't know what you mean.

GREG

Forget it. I think Robby and Giovanni are taking Maria's two friends. I don't think they put out, but I guess they liked the guys. Giovanni and I don't talk about what his sister and I do. He's OK with his sister dating me, as long as I don't talk about what we do. She's a good lay, but that's all she is to me. Besides, I think she's engaged to some guy in Florida.

MARK

You're making me horny, just talking about doing it.

GREG

Yeah, me, too.

MARK

You want to you know . . . go somewhere and let's do it . . . you know . . . jack-off?

GREG

Well, I did it before I got up this morning. Then again while I was taking my shower, but I can do it again. Yeah, sure, let's do it.

MARK

Let's just fucking do it then! I don't know why, but it's a lot better . . . you know . . . . doing it when somebody else is watching.

(In Greg's Basement)
GREG

Have you ordered your graduations invitations yet?

GIOVANNI

I'm not ordering any. Why order invitations when there is no one to send them to?

GREG

There's your sister and your mom. And you could send them to all our parents. I know my mom and dad will be at our graduation, and if you send them one, I'm sure they'll give you a graduation gift. Besides, I'm sure your dad will want one for a souvenir. He must be proud of you for finishing high school.

GIOVANNI

Yeah! Right! I doubt if he even knows that I am going to graduate this year. He thinks I'm dumb as dirt, and he doesn't even care whether I go to school. My mom won't come. My sister is getting married in June, so she will not be up, too busy planning her wedding. My dad, Greg, he's . . . . well, he's got problems. He drinks, he can't hold a job, and something happened between him and my mom that caused them to split. I don't know exactly what it was, but I do know he was not at home very much. He said my sister is a whore and he thinks I'm dumb, sorry and ugly.

GREG

Why do you say that?

GIOVANNI

Why does *he* say that?

GREG

Well, I don't think those things about you. You're smart, dependable, and damn good looking!

GIOVANNI

That's the first time anyone ever told me I look good. Especially a boy. Anyway, my dad won't come to see me graduate. And that's OK by me. It's just as well that he doesn't, because he would probably be drunk. I'm not going through the graduation exercises anyway. I'm going to ask the counselor to just mail it to me.

GREG

What? Not walking with us to get your diploma? I don't understand . . .

GIOVANNI

It's just money wasted. You know, renting caps and gowns, buying invitations, graduation pictures, year books . . . . all that stuff is just money thrown away. Money my dad won't give me.

GREG

Maybe we will all think that, someday, but . . . . well, right now, it's important, just something we all do. It makes memories, and later in life it will be fun to be reminded of the good times we had during our high school days. Our own kids can look at our yearbooks and laugh at how weird we looked.

GIOVANNI

I'm not having any kids. So far, being a kid hasn't had many good memories, and in a few weeks the so called "good times" of high school will be over. Then what? Nothing! At least as far as I can see now, just plain nothing. I have no idea what I'm going to do.

GREG

We've had some good times, Giovanni. Mark, Robby and I consider you our best friend. You've only been here a few months, but it's almost like you've been here with us since our elementary school days. And we've had some fun, the ball games, the dances, movies, riding around town, fishing, swimming . . . . getting a little nookie now and then . . .

GIOVANNI

You! You get nookie, Greg! I don't. My hand is all I ever get! And I doubt if Robby and Mark ever do it. They talk about it a lot, but I doubt if they ever actually get any. It's just talk. I don't know what their problem is, but mine is that my skin is too dark or not dark enough. Robby has light skin, but he is still a Black boy, so he should get laid. Mark's problem is that he just doesn't try with girls! The only way I'm not a virgin, is because I use my own hand on a daily basis! And Mark . . . . well, he's nice looking, with his big blue eyes, his blond hair and those dimples, he should be getting laid as much as you. But he's got a problem.

GREG

Wait a minute! Are you saying that you think Mark is *gay?*

GIOVANNI

Gay, queer, fag, pansy . . . . Whatever!

GREG

Watch it, fellow! He's been my friend since second grade. If he was that way, I would know! So you just watch your mouth. And even if he were, he'd still be my friend!

GIOVANNI

Cool it! It's alright by me if he is. I don't give a flying fuck what he likes to do.

GREG

Then, just shut your mouth about Mark, Giovanni!

GIOVANNI

So, now I guess I'm not one of the "gang" . . . no longer one of the "good old boys" just because I think Mark is queer. Well, fuck you! anyway, Greg! And fuck Mark and Robby, too! I don't need your fucking friendship! (he leaves, as Robby and Mark arrive)

ROBBY

What's happening? What's he mad about?

GREG

It's nothing. He's just upset about graduation. I don't think he has the money for all the expenses. That and the fact that his dad won't come to see him receive his diploma. He's going to have it mailed to him.

MARK

Hey, we can help him. I've got a little money saved up from my job. And my dad is so surprised, and even happy, I think, that I am going to graduate, I think I can talk him into giving me a little more money than I really need for my class ring. Won't be the first time I've lied to him. Robby, you always have money. Can you help?

GREG

I can put in a little, too. Well, great! We'll just do it.

MARK

And I know his dad. I can talk to him, and I think he'll come to graduation, if I ask him.

GREG

His family must treat him like shit. Except for his sister, she seems to be really close to him.

MARK

Yeah. His dad is a drunk. Can't keep a job. Never has anything nice to say about Giovanni.

GREG

Sounds like you know his dad? How?

MARK

How what? He did some yard work for my dad a few times. He lives in a trailer court. Typical trailer trash! I make deliveries. It's part of my job. And I used to drive him home sometimes when he finished work in our yard. They don't even have a car.

ROBBY

He talks about his granddad sometimes. I think he lives in California. In his younger day, his granddad was an actor . . . had two or three bit parts in some movies, at least that's what Giovanni claims.

GREG

He never talks about personal things with me. Never tells me anything about his family nor his life before he came here. His sister has told me more about him than he has.

MARK

Well, he knows I can relate to his family and their problems. Even though our families are so different, we have some of the same dysfunctional problems. He's met my family. My dad makes more money than his, but I have to beg for what I get. He has already told me he will not pay for my college education. Like I said, he thinks it would be a poor investment, because he thinks I would flunk out . . . . and I probably would! Anyway, I don't want his money. I can make it without his help. My brother did. I don't ever want to be obligated to anyone, nor responsible for anyone except myself. Well, now I have to go and earn some money, so I'm out of here. See you guys later, (he leaves)

ROBBY

When did the discussion become all about **him**? I thought we were talking about Giovanni's problems. Anyway, where does Mark work. He doesn't spend as much time with us as he used to. I thought he works at a fast-food place, but I have never seen him in one. He says he makes deliveries as part of his job. Maybe that's why I never see him at work.

GREG

I think he works part-time at a hamburger place, and then he does some little odd jobs . . . at odd times! He says he's trying to save enough money to get out of here when he graduates.

(Giovanni returns to basement)

ROBBY

How's it going, man? (Giovanni does not answer) 'S' up? . . . . speak, ass, mouth won't!

GIOVANNI

Nothings up. I'm just not in such a good mood.

GREG

If you're still mad with me, just get over it. If you came to apologize, then I accept the apology. We're friends, Giovanni, and friends get mad with each other sometimes, but we get over it quick. We love you, man.

ROBBY

That goes for me, too, ... for Mark, as well. We all love you. You're one of us.

GIOVANNI

Thanks! I really mean it. I've never had a guy tell me . . . that, before. In fact, If anyone ever told me that, I don't remember it. Right at this particular time, it sounds good . . . . to have friends that will say that.

GREG

So, we're OK. OK?

GIOVANNI

Right, we're OK. Where is Mark? Where did he go?

ROBBY

He has an after-school job.

GIOVANNI

I was walking home from the grocery store the other day, and I was almost sure that I saw Mark drive away from our . . . mobile home. He was in his dad's car. I didn't even know that he knows where I live. I've tried to keep all of you from knowing that I live in a mobile home. And we've got creepy neighbors.

GREG

He said that sometimes he gives your dad a ride home after he finishes working in his dad's yard. And that he makes deliveries to your house. And, Giovanni, we really don't care where you live. It doesn't matter.

GIOVANNI

My dad has never worked in anyone's yard, not even our own. And we have never had deliveries made to our house. I have to walk to the store to get groceries, and my dad goes there only when he buys his beer.

ROBBY

Giovanni, we don't know what happens in your home. But it doesn't matter. We are your friends. We all have some kind of family problems, but we guys are always here for each other. That's why friendships are important. And we are friends, that's something that will never change.

GREG

That's right. You trusted us enough to become our friend? So just remember that trust! Anyway, why did you like us? We're not the most popular guys in school.

GIOVANNI

I don't know. I guess one reason was that I knew you were all straight. I never had friends before. Once, when I was in junior high, I tried to be friends with a boy, and he called me a "queer" and a "pussy", just because I asked him to come over to my house to visit. I never tried to have friends after that. Every time another guy got friendly with me, I wondered if he was having those ideas about me, you know, if he thought I was gay and that he was, too. So, I always backed away from friendships. But I could tell that you guys are straight, and when you asked me to come over and play ball that first time, well, I was really happy.

(Greg winks at Robby, and they are all over Giovanni, kissing and groping him in playful teasing)

GREG

Just shows you how wrong you can be! We're all gay, and we want your body!

ROBBY

We've been wanting your cute ass ever since we met you!

GIOVANNI

Stop it, you fucking idiots! (he's loving the attention, because he knows they are teasing and that it is all in fun. They are all laughing. They stop and all sit quietly for a few moments)

ROBBY

Damn! That almost made me horny! Giovanni, you would have made a cute girl! I wish you were. I would take you here and now!

GIOVANNI

Shut up! (but obviously found the remarks complimentary)

GREG

No, he's right . . . . you sure turned me on! And I think your third leg has grown some since I took measurements. I felt that woody you got on. Man you have to admit, you liked being felt up.

GIOVANNI

You crazy shit! I never got a hard-on! (laughing and a bit embarrassed). You fucking shits! You're both fucking crazy!

(Fishing, at the Pond)

GREG

Did you bring it?

GIOVANNI

Yes, it's in the ice chest.

GREG

Don't tell the others yet. We'll build a campfire later, then surprise them.

GIOVANNI

After all the preaching and lecturing you've done, it will definitely be a surprise! Where are they?

GREG

They are looking for wood to build the campfire, for after it gets dark.

GIOVANNI

Did you bring the fishing poles?

GREG

Sure. They're down by the lake. Got plenty of crickets, too. Here come Mark and Robby now. Great! You found plenty of wood.

ROBBY

Yeah. It's dry, too. Should be easy to start a fire, (to Giovanni) How did you get here?

GIOVANNI

A neighbor dropped me off by the roadside. Is everybody ready to fish?

MARK

Not yet. Let's go for a swim first. The water should be really warm.

ROBBY

We didn't bring bathing suits. I thought we were coming to fish.

MARK

Since when has that stopped us. We can go skinny dipping. Even Giovanni is not shy anymore.

GREG

Nobody's shy, Mark. But we fish first, then swim. If we go into the water now, we'll scare the fish away, (all put fishing poles into the water)

GIOVANNI

This will probably be my last time fishing with you guys.

MARK

That's right. You'll be leaving for California the day after graduation, won't you?

GIOVANNI

Yes, my granddad is expecting me the first of June. But how did you know when I'm leaving?

MARK

I guess your dad might have mentioned it to me. I don't know.

ROBBY

Hey! Look at my cork! I'm getting a nibble.

GREG

Yank! Now's the time to yank!

MARK

That's a big one. Robby's always the first to catch one. Sometimes he's the only one to catch one.

GREG

But it's like I always say . . . . it's not who does it first, but who does it the most that counts.

GIOVANNI
I'm guessing that is some more of your sex talk . . . . about your *drivel* Can't we even fish without having to hear that you are bigger, better, more . . . . hotter . . . . or whatever . . .

GREG
Quiet! I'm getting a bite now.

GIOVANNI
Bite me!

GREG
Unzip it and I will, asshole!

GIOVANNI
Fuck you, fuck-face! (they are just having fun)

(Around the campfire)

MARK
This is great! I still can't believe that you brought beer, Greg.

GREG
I didn't. Giovanni brought it. But it was my idea.

ROBBY
When did you decide we could do this. We've never . . . **Why** did you decide we could do this? If my dad knew I was drinking beer, he . . . I don't know what he would do!

GREG
It's just a one-time thing. I thought that we need this one time to remember before we graduate and go our separate ways.

MARK

It's a great idea, whatever the reason. And I'll have to admit now, that I've had beer before. But I've never got drunk. Tonight I want to get fucking drunk!

GREG

No, Mark! Just a couple of cans for each of us. No more. Nobody's going to get drunk.

MARK

I am. I'm going to get stinking drunk. I just want to see what it's like . . . just one time.

ROBBY

You're already well on the way to being drunk, Mark. That's number six for you.

GREG

Mark, if you're not used to it, it doesn't take much to make you drunk. And it can sneak up on you. You'll be drunk before you know it.

ROBBY

Then you had better stop now, because you are downing them pretty fast yourself. In fact, you've had more cans than Mark.

MARK

What the hell are you doing? Are you counting how many everybody is drinking? Just leave us the hell alone. We'll drink as much as we like.

GREG

(he is drunk) Shut up, Mark! You can't talk to my good friend, Robby, like that.

MARK

(he is drunk) You shut up! You always take up for Robby. You don't ever take my side. You like him better than you do me.

GREG

I'm sorry, Mark! I love you, man. You know I love you!

MARK

Yeah, I know. I'm sorry I said that, Robby . . . . I'm sorry, Greg, my good, good friend. I love you, too.

GREG

No. I mean it, Mark! I *really love* you. (Mark is asleep, or passing out)

GIOVANNI

Both of you shut up before you make me puke! (he does)

ROBBY

Come on, Giovanni. Let's go for another swim and I'll help you get washed off.

(morning, driving home)

GREG

What in the hell was I thinking? . . . . telling you to bring beer! I'll have to try to slip into the house and get to my room . . . . God! I hope my mom and dad don't see me like this!

ROBBY

My parents probably have the police out searching for my body. They'll be so glad to see that I'm alive . . . . then they'll fucking *kill* me! They are going to be so disappointed in me.

GIOVANNI

My dad is going to kill me . . . . for stealing his beer! Now, I wish I hadn't. My head is aching, and I puked all over myself last night. Thanks, Robby for taking my clothes off and washing me off in the creek.

MARK

What else did you two do, after we went to sleep? My dad is going to be so proud of me. I've finally done something that measures up to what his expectations of his teen-age son should be. So, you two had fun after Greg and I went to sleep? This damn hang-over is no fun, I can tell you that!

(In School Hallway)
ROBBY

Can you believe that! Even twelve-year olds are doing it. I didn't even go through puberty until I was fourteen.

MARK

Yes, Greg and I well remember that. We were there your first time, and we thought you were having a seizure. But, you know, you can actually do it before you hit puberty. I was eight and my cousin Beth was eleven when we did it.

ROBBY

You did your own cousin? That's just sick, man!

MARK

I didn't do her. She did me. I didn't even know where to put it. She had to guide me in. That was my one and only time. Technically, I think I still qualify as a virgin.

ROBBY

Mark, tell me truthfully, have you really never had the opportunity, or is it because you are saving yourself for the right woman.

MARK

The right woman, Mark, would be *any* woman that would give it to me!

GIOVANNI

Mark, you are a good-looking guy, decent enough, good personality when you're not in one of your bad moods . . . . Maybe you're a bit retarded, but not enough for it to be a problem getting a girl, I mean, after all, there are many equally retarded girls all over the campus. So, I'm just wondering, what is your problem?

MARK

What problem? What do you mean? You think I have a problem, just because . . . . Maybe *you're* the one with a problem!

GIOVANNI

Yes, I think you have a problem. You're not getting girls. That's a problem. Could it be because, just maybe, *you don't want one?*

GREG

Giovanni, don't go there! Just don't say another word!

MARK

Oh, he's going to say something alright He's going to say just exactly what he's hinting at! It's not the first time.

GIOVANNI

Forget it.

MARK

Forget you! (Mark leaves)

ROBBY

(after a minute) So, anyway, Mr. Adams says that a high percentage of twelve-year olds are doing it. Next week our final chapter in the health book deals with AIDS. Mr. Adams says it's important for us to study it diligently. Giovanni, now that I think about it, I have not seen you chasing many girls, yourself. Do you have a secret that you want to share with us?

(Playing Tennis)

MARK

I just want to try it. Just once, to see what it's like. I hear the other kids talking about it . . . . kids younger than we are, and I want to do it, too.

GREG

No! Not just "no", but *"hell no"*!

MARK

Greg, you're not the boss of me! You can't stop me, man! It's my decision . . . . it's my business! I just thought that you might want to try it with me, but just forget it. I never should have mentioned it to you. If you don't want to smoke one with me, *then . . . . just fucking forget about it!* It's none of your business, unless you want in.

GREG

The hell you say! What do you mean it's none of my business? We're best friends, and I'm not going to stand by and watch I'm just not going to let you do it, that's all!

MARK

You can't stop me.

ROBBY

Yes, we can. We can stop you, Mark.

GIOVANNI

Mark, I've seen guys, lots of them . . . . doing that stuff. You're too smart for that. I know I've called you retarded before, but I didn't mean it . . . . well, maybe a little, but the point is; it only takes one smoke to get you hooked. It stinks, it's expensive, and it can ruin your health. It can ruin your life. And is it really worth it, when it can also take away your sex drive, whatever direction it's driving in? But, guys, I say let him go ahead and do it . . . .

MARK

Why are all of you getting so hyper over a little thing like me smoking a joint? It's nothing.

GREG

Mark, it's not ***nothing***! It's very much something, it's a bad habit to start, but it's more than that, it's breaking a trust, a promise. A promise that we made to each other as friends. A responsibility to each other, or have you forgotten?

MARK

OK, just forget it. Forget I ever mentioned it to you.

ROBBY

No. We're not going to forget it. We have an agreement.

MARK

What? What agreement? That we are going to be each other's guardian angels for the rest of our fucking lives? Well, I have no intention of letting you tell me what I can and can't do anymore.

GREG

We agreed that none of us would drink, nor smoke. And, that if one of us tried it, the other two would beat the crap out of him.

MARK

We were in the fucking fourth grade! We were kids! We're not in that place anymore. We, ... at least I am grown up now. I'm my own person; my own man! I'm an individual, separate from you guys, even if we are still friends. I'm not like you, and I don't want to be like anyone else.

GREG
So, it was important when we were ten years old, but it's not important anymore?

MARK
We're grown up, Greg. We all have to face that fact. You cannot boss me around anymore.

GREG
(calmly) If you light up that joint, Mark, I'm prepared to beat the crap out of you. ***Do you fucking understand that language?***

ROBBY
And I'm prepared to help him, Mark. That's how much we love you.

GIOVANNI
If beating the crap out of you is what it takes, Mark, I think you're worth it. Count me in, too.

MARK
You guys really mean it don't you. I mean, you do care that much about me.

GREG
Damn right! After all these years together, did you doubt it?

MARK
I do remember the pact we made. And I won't break it, at least not now. But it's not because I'm afraid of any one of you or all of you together! It's because you care about . . . . well, it's just because . . . . (he has tears in his eyes)

GREG
Great, because I don't want to taste munchings on those sweet lips the next time I fucking ***kiss*** you. Like now! (The three friends

are all over Mark, kissing him and fondling him. It's teasing, and Mark loves it. All are laughing)

GIOVANNI

OK, you guys. That's enough. Leave him alone before he gets a hard on. Greg, I would like to point out at this time that you should just remember who it was that suggested we all have beer that night at the lake.

(Swimming at creek)

GREG

So, did Mr. Adams explain it all? You know, about AIDS?

ROBBY

Yeah, I guess he did. He says that he has to be careful about how much he can say to us, you know, there are set guidelines which he has to follow. Some more explicit words, he's not allowed to use.

GREG

I've read that some people who have AIDS, or who are HIV positive, have to take hundreds of pills every week, day after day for the rest of their lives in order to live.

ROBBY

Mr. Adams says that it's not as bad as it used to be. Medications have been combined into one pill, and better, more affective treatments have been discovered. The problem remains that some people cannot afford medication and others don't even get tested.

MARK

What else did he discuss?

ROBBY

Emotional impact on the victim as well as the family of the guy who gets it. And insurance problems. He says that it's important to be tested soon after you do something that could cause you to get it. And he talked about how you can get it. Well, actually he discussed *around* the issue of how you can get it. Something about mixing body fluids. That's about all.

MARK

They never tell it all. I'll bet you he did not tell the class *exactly how* those body fluids get mixed.

ROBBY

He said, you know, by doing stuff. Sex stuff.

MARK

What kind of "sex stuff? I'll bet he did not tell that to the class.

ROBBY

Just about any kind, I guess. But the main thing is to not do it, he said. And if you do, then use a condom.

GREG

Yeah, just don't do it is the only safe way to not get it. Nothing prevents it like abstinence, so they say.

GIOVANNI

Yeah, but who's going to "just not do it"? Everybody does it. Except maybe Mark! But my question is: how can you use a condom when you're doing oral sex?

MARK

Well, duh! You just put a condom on his penis, just like if you are fucking a girl.

GIOVANNI

I am talking about when you are doing oral sex on a girl, you nit-wit! (they all look at Mark)

MARK

Well, Mr. Adams is the expert. Why didn't you ask him?

ROBBY

I was too shy. I don't want anyone in class to know that I'm so inexperienced that I don't know how to perform oral sex on a girl.

GIOVANNI

I'll bet Mr. Adams has experienced just about everything. Mark, why don't you go and ask him . . . . in private. Maybe he will explain it all to you in detail, maybe he will even demonstrate some things for you.

GREG

Shut up, Giovanni. You know that Mr. and Mrs. Adams seem to be a happily married couple. He'd never do anything outside of his marriage.

(The Prom)

MARK

I never said I could dance. I only consented to come to the prom because my mom said you would enjoy it.

BETH

Always a bride's maid always a wallflower always a blind date, with some desperate creature. The story of my life! And finally it has come to this, my first time I'm actually taken to a prom is with my younger cousin!

MARK

Beth, be thankful for favors, and this is not a small one! Trust me, I don't even want to be here, but at least you are here. You can finally say you went to a prom.

BETH

Oh, I've been to proms before. I've just never had anyone take me to one before. The other "plain" girls and I always go together and stand around the wall together. And we make stupid remarks about how pretty the dresses look on the pretty girls, and how slutty the dresses look on the sluts. Knowing all the time that we were wishing we were going to get laid by the sexy guys that are going to take their dates to a motel after the prom is over.

MARK

Well, don't look now, but I think you are going to get lucky! Mr. Stephens is the Science teacher, and I don't think he's coming over to hit on me. He already has, and trust me, I'm still a virgin just like you.

BETH

I didn't say that I'm still a virgin. I simply said that . . . . ***Oh my God!*** He is looking me over, and he's coming over here. I don't care how old he is, if he asks me to dance, I'm dancing . . . . if I don't pass out first. If he tries to kiss me . . . . I'm kissing! If he as much as hints about a motel, you go on home alone, because I'm losing my virginity tonight! But . . . . he's probably looking at someone behind me, or hoping he'll luck up with you this time.

MARK

He's looking directly at you, Beth. And I know that look. I can see he's got a backup of semen, because it's popping out of his eyes and ears! (Mr. Stephens approaches) Hello, Mr. Stephens. Beautiful prom, isn't it. I helped decorate for it.

Mr. STEPHENS

I know. You little artsy boys did a great job with the decorations. Who is your mature friend. I'm sure she's not your girlfriend. Cousin? Sister?

BETH

I'm Beth. Mark's older cousin, and I'm not really his date. Since he couldn't get a real date, I consented to make an appearance with him. I could leave at any time now.

Mr. STEPHENS

Well, how about that. I was just leaving, also. I could give you a lift. I'll just wait outside, (he leaves)

MARK

Oh, yes. You are going to get laid tonight. Just remember that I could have had him first. He is one of my rejects. Enjoy!

BETH

I don't give a fat rat's ass how many you have or have not rejected. This is one night I ain't going to be rejected. Thanks, Mark. It's the most beautiful prom I ever saw. I'll talk to you sometime next week . . . if I'm back home by then, (she leaves)

MARK

Great! I'm out of here, too.

GREG

Hey, Mark! Having fun? This is a great night. Everybody seems happy and excited.

MARK

Yeah! Everybody's happy. You should know, because you've danced with every girl here, (he leaves)

GREG

Come back! I'll even dance with you!

(After leaving the prom, Greg and Mark drive to the lake. They lie on the deck where boats are anchored)

GREG

Forget the prom. I didn't want to go anymore than you did. Karen went with that guy she's been seeing, and I really did not want a date. Girls are just not on my mind right at this time.

MARK

I know. You're still hoping for that scholarship to The University of Alabama. Stop worrying, I'm sure you'll get it.

GREG

Just think! Two more weeks and we're out of here. If I get the scholarship, I'll leave immediately for the campus for summer practice.

MARK

And Giovanni will be leaving for California in about three weeks. Robby will be leaving in the fall, for Birmingham Southern.

GREG

And you, Mark . . . . What? You still have not told us about any definite plans. You need to be especially nice to your parents. Maybe there's still a chance that they will finance your way through college.

MARK

That ship has already sailed. I missed the boat. I have never been the ideal son, and the accumulation of disobedient behaviors, the ones I got caught in, anyway, have built up into a mountain of . . . . well, big fat, loud "7W?'s! Greg, the truth is, I don't know yet what I am going to do. Like my brother, I will probably get out on my own in a few weeks. The problem is, my brother was good looking, and he was able to rely on the "kindness of friends". Still does, after five years. I'm not that good-looking. I'm going to have to rely on my own imagination about how to survive.

GREG

Man, don't sell yourself short! You're the cutest guy in school. At least to me you are. I've always been envious of your blue eyes, your blond curls and pearly-girly fair skin. I hate it that we can't go off to college together, all of us. Mark, I am really worried about you. We've been like brothers since the first grade. I love you. We've always planned to go off to college and live together, enjoy the parties, the games, all of it.

MARK

Greg, I lost that dream a long time ago. I don't know when we will ever see each other again. But what you said about loving me, well, you must know that I love you, too. I always have, (they lie in silence for a few minutes)

GREG

(Mark's hand is on Greg's crotch. He unzips Greg's pants, and begins to grope) Hey, man, what are you doing?

MARK

I . . . . I don't know . . . . I just . . . . Does it feel good? I can tell it does!

GREG

Yeah! But, Mark, I . . . .

MARK

I'll stop if you want me to. Are you sure . . . . I mean, that it feels as good to you as it does to me?

GREG

Yeah, but when I said I love you, well, I don't think I'm like that.

MARK

Like what? Oh. Well, I don't think I am either.

GREG

Well . . . . OK, then.

(Graduation night)

GIOVANNI

Now that it's all over. Too late, I wish that I had tried to excel in something, just anything, so that I could say I was good at something back in my high-school days.

ROBBY

My parents would not let me play basketball or do any sports. They thought I might get hurt. They were so protective of me that I couldn't even have a bicycle. Greg taught me how to ride his. What would you have wanted to do in high school that you didn't do?

GIOVANNI

A swimmer, I guess. No, what I really wanted to do was to be an actor like my grandfather. I was in a few plays before I came here. Once, I was in *"The King and I",* at a regular, paying theatre. I really got paid, not much, but it was enough to make it a professional performance. I didn't get to talk, I just marched in with the Siamese kids and sang with them.

ROBBY

When you get to California with your granddad, you should go for it! I'm happy that Mark passed his exams and is graduating.

I'm glad that your dad is here tonight, too. You don't like Mark, do you?

GIOVANNI

He's OK. I just think he's gay, and I think he should have been truthful to us about it.

ROBBY

He's probably not gay, Giovanni! And even if he is, so what? No one should have to tell anyone else about his sexual preferences. Did he ever "hit" on you? If not, then you have no reason to say that about him.

GIOVANNI

No, he never actually came on to me, but I've seen him looking at me, you know, when we're all naked.

ROBBY

That's just what guys do. We all do, you know, look at each other and compare. I've looked at you, too. You're big, well hung, and you look a little different, you know kind of semi-cut. You've compared, too. Admit it! You've looked at us when we go swimming without our bathing suits. Mark has only compared. You're bigger than he is, he looks at yours. It's called _envy._ He looks at Greg, too. I have, and you have, also. I've seen you gawking at his big piece.

GIOVANNI

You're right. And it really has not bothered me. I guess I just wanted him to tell me if he's gay. It might have made us closer . . . . friends, you know. But it really does not matter now. I'll be gone next week. Robby, I'll never forget my months here with you guys. Thanks.

ROBBY

For what?

GIOVANNI

I don't know. For a lot of stuff. For paying for my class ring, renting my cap and gown, my invitations, for Mark getting my father to come tonight, whatever he had to do to make that happen most of all, thanks for being the only friends I have ever had.

(Greg and Mark, Graduation Night)

GREG

So. Mark, the time has finally come. It's all over but the shouting.

MARK

No, it's just now beginning. At least for me, life is just beginning.

GREG

You once said that you would not miss anything about high school. Do you still feel that way?

MARK

No. I'll miss you. That's all. And maybe the other guys, too, sometimes, I guess. But mostly I'll just miss you. I appreciate and remember only one teacher out of all the teachers here, because he gave me so many "second chances" that I can't count all of them so, I graduate. And now we all leave with our memories, most of which I hope to soon forget.

GREG

I'm sorry for you. For the fact that you had so many unpleasant experiences here. I have memories that I will be happy to recall throughout my lifetime.

MARK

Great! Good for you! (after a pause) Greg, do you remember that night after the prom? When you and I went out to the pond. Was that one of your good memories'." I want to tell you before we leave, that I'm sorry about that . . . . I mean, about what happened . . .

GREG

Don't be. I mean, don't be sorry. I'm not. I'm not sorry about any of the experiences we have shared together. You and I have been friends, almost brothers, since before we started to school in the first grade. And Robby, too. And then, during this year, Giovanni as well.

MARK

Yeah. I know. I always liked Robby more than he knew more than I let him know.

GREG

Everything that happened between us, the great experiences as well as the unpleasant ones, is what has made us what we are today. I don't regret any of it. I don't want you to leave with any regrets, at least not about our relationships.

MARK

I don't think I have any regrets that will get in the way of my future. I know I have no regrets about you and me. You know, I wanted to *be you*. If I couldn't be you, I wanted to be more like you. I couldn't. So, I just wanted to be as close to you as I could be.

GREG

We will always be close. It will always be that way.

MARK

Greg, it's already slipping away, here, now . . . . as we graduate tonight!

GREG

Mark, it can't slip away! I love you, man!

MARK

Don't you think I know that, Greg? And I love you, too. But sometimes love itself can cause regrets . . . . regrets for things that are said, but also for things that are not said; will never be said!

GREG

Then, Mark, always remember to express what you truly feel. It could unlock doors that are rusting away because they were never opened.

MARK

The music is starting. We need to line up with the others and join the march. It's the last time I will ever march to someone else's music.

GREG

Let's shake hands, before we line up with the others.

MARK

Shake hands to "Goodbye"?

GREG

No! I don't know to what? Maybe to seal a promise . . . . a promise to *something*! (they shake hands, briefly, but tightly)

MARK

It wasn't long enough . . . . holding your hand, I mean.

GREG

Nothing good ever lasts long enough fuck it all!

EPILOGUE

GREG

I did not receive a football scholarship to the University of Alabama. Discouraged, I decided to delay my entrance into college, and took a job at the local Wal-Mart instead, while I waited for some clue as to what I would do with my life. After a couple of years, I was transferred to a store in Mobile, Alabama, where I was trained as an assistant manager. I married and soon became the father of twin boys. I like my life . . . . most of the time.

ROBBY

After graduating from high school, my parents insisted that I go on a Summer trip to Europe. They thought my study in personal relations, after I returned, would be more meaningful, if I observed and lived a few months in another culture. I love Paris. I got a French girl pregnant, and I'm still undecided about what to do when my parents stop sending money. Maybe I will go back home and make my parents happy by going to college. Maybe I'll stay here and marry Collette, or maybe I'll just drift on down to Italy for awhile.

GIOVANNI

The guys really proved their friendship. They not only paid all of my graduation expenses, but also bought my flight ticket to LA. And my dad really made me happy by showing up at my graduation. He was on time, dressed well and ***sober!*** Although I still have not figured that one out, I know that Mark had something to do with it. I try not to think too much about it. My grandfather really needed me here in LA, and he has helped me a lot also. Recently, he brought to some important person's attention, my dark hair and tan skin, not to mention my green eyes (due to contact lens). As a result, I have a photo session set up and have scheduled an audition for a walk-on part in a movie. Who knows what lies ahead, or what I will have to do to become an actor.

MARK

Giovanni's dad showed up at graduation. It required an extra blow-job on my part, but it was worth it to see the smile on Giovanni's face at seeing his dad there. Sometime during the Summer, we all just drifted apart. I'm working nights, part-time, with a cleaning service, while I attend classes during the day at U.A.B. I avoid all the math courses I can. I really enjoy my art and drama classes. They are a result of Giovanni's influence on me. I am sure he never knew how much I admired him and looked up to him. My late night hours are usually spent in the gay bars on Southside. That's where I met Dirk. We live together.

A Dream
For Every Heart

By
Robert Bertrand

A DREAM FOR EVERY HEART

A morning in May should not be so cool, not here in Columbiana, Alabama. However, Esther could remember through the years when early May nights on the porch would require a sweater, or one of her knitted shawls. After dressing, she made her bed, brushed out her long gray hair, knotted it behind her neck and walked to the window. As she looked from her second-floor bedroom, she saw that it had rained during the night. She had heard the thunder. It had reminded her to pray. She had thanked God for this big, old house which she had hated all of her life, but for which she was thankful. She had heard that there were people in Birmingham who were "homeless" and that they slept under the bridges and overpasses, covering themselves with boxes, rags and old carpets. So, even though she did not like the house, she was happy that at least she was not trying to sleep under some damp, noisy bridge in the city. She was all the more thankful for the house when there was rain, thunder and lightening, which was something else she did not like. From her window she could see that the grass, the vegetable garden, the leaves on the trees and the rose bushes below sparkled with remaining raindrops. It was a beautiful, cool morning.

Esther Lou and her sisters, Lilly Mae and Mabel Katherine had played happily in the shades of large old oak and pecan trees when they were little girls. Esther was the oldest. Mabel was the youngest. Lilly, the middle sister, was the prettiest. People often said so, and Mabel would pout every time she would hear, "Oh, that Lilly Mae, she is the pretty one in that family.".

Mabel had left home to pursue an acting career when she finished high school. Indeed, she claimed to be an actress after she had arrived in New York City. No one back in Alabama knew if it were true, nor did anyone care.

Lilly had married Calvin and moved into a small apartment in Birmingham. Her twins were born seven months later. Billy was born two years after that. Before he was a year old, Lilly had died. Calvin had found it necessary to move in with his sister-in-law, so that she could help with the children. He had to work. Esther needed the financial support this arrangement gave her. She learned to love her niece and nephews, but raising her sister's children had not been exactly what she had wanted in life.

Mabel had come home to several funerals and a few weddings. The funerals, besides her sister's, were those of the older generation which included her parents and an assortment of aunts and uncles. The weddings were various cousins and a few friends who thought it nice to have a New York City actress in their weddings. But now Mabel's visits back to the old home place had become infrequent. She still held half ownership in the property, but her "acting career" was in New York, and that was where she wanted to be.

Esther never married. She had never had a boyfriend. There had never been time for such things as parties and dating, she always said. The truth was that no man had found her attractive. If John Morrison had asked her, she would have made time to go out with him. But he never asked. And so her life had been spent helping to raise Lilly and Calvin's three children, caring for the ill and dying, and burying the dead.

JOSEPH

"I didn't eat the grits." He stated. "I just didn't want the damn grits."

Carlos pondered this for longer than a minute, with a confused expression that overshadowed his exotic, extreme good looks. This confused look was often on his face, always reminding Joe that Carlos' star shown ever-so-slightly less bright than the average star in the sky. Sometimes, it seemed to Joe that Carlos' reactions to most situations were just plain stupid. In fact, Joe wondered how such a beautiful, brown body with an extremely handsome face and rich, black hair, could have so little ability in the head section to figure out the simple things in life.

Finally, Carlos asked, "You left home because you didn't like grits?"

"I left home because I hated grits. My Aunt Esther said, 'Here's your grits.' And I just sat and stared at my bowl of grits. But I didn't see the grits. All I could see was my life. I hated my life not my family, just my life *with* my family. I hated that damn big, old house. I hated the farm, even the animals. And I love animals, I just hated those because they were ours. I even hated the swimming hole where Billy and me used to go skinny dipping when the days were so damn hot. We used to slip away from the cotton fields, cross over the cow pasture to the woods where the creek ran, pull off our clothes and jump in. It was the coolest, cleanest water in the whole world. I loved it back then. That's where I taught Billy . . . . things. Those were fun days. But then I grew up and I hated my life there." Joe finished.

"Sounds pretty good to me. I mean, like a good life. Why would you want to leave it?" Carlos' smile had returned. It was a smile that could always change that stupid look of a serious nature back into the beautiful face that Joe found so exciting.

"Like I said, I hated it. I pushed the bowl of grits away from me and left." Joe said, and he wanted to say more, but it took a few seconds for him to summon the courage to say it. To say it even to Carlos, as close as they had become, was not easy for him. But he continued, "I remember Aunt Esther just standing by the stove looking at me with a puzzled stare. As I left the kitchen, Billy came through the doorway, still buttoning up his shirt, still half asleep. We passed through the doorway, stopping just long enough to face eye-to-eye. That moment is what I remember most about my leaving. We just looked at each other without saying a word, but our eyes were asking a simple question . . . . 'Why?' It's a question I still ask myself. Maybe he's still asking it, too. Or maybe he has already figured out the answer."

Carlos said, "Well, if you had not left that morning, you and I would never have met. And neither of us could have made it alone."

Joe knew he was right. Carlos had a fantastic voice, but Joe had to make all the decisions, plans, audition appointments, and sometimes he even had to tell Carlos how a certain song should be sung. Joe could sing with Carlos, but not solo. He played the guitar a little, but his musical ability was as weak as Carlos' mental ability. Three chords and an occasional extra thrown-in strum was all he could do. Arranging Carlos' singing to fit his limited picking ability was necessary in order for them to get gigs. Sometimes the gigs were short and far between. Street performances would bring in a few dollars for food, mainly due to Carlos' good looks. Young girls and old gays would drop in a buck or two now and then, along with a name and telephone number.

A November night brought a Northwestern cold front into Tennessee. Fortunately the two young men had made enough money that day for a good meal and a room for the night. The next day, Joe would have to make some plans for them to move farther South to a warmer climate. But tonight, in a warm bed, they would enjoy doing what they usually did each night since they met two years earlier.

LOUANNE

Louanne had delivered her valedictory speech well, went to a hang-out with a few friends, and then went home early. Her family was waiting for her. Her proud father, her Aunt Esther and Billy. Joseph had left home after having dropped out of school after the tenth grade, two years earlier. Louanne, his twin sister, had always been number one in her class, from kindergarten through graduation. Louanne's achievements partially made up for the disappointment Calvin felt for Joe's lack of interest in study. Playing the guitar was his only interest, but after years of practice, he was still no good with the instrument. His family would scatter hither, thither and yon when he would pick up the instrument and go to the wide front veranda to practice his chords.

"I wish Joe had graduated with me tonight." Louanne said, taking the glass of iced tea and the cake which her Aunt Esther had made for this occasion.

"Don't mention his name in front of me. Not in this house. Not tonight. Tonight is yours and ours, not his." Her father remarked.

Aunt Esther said, proudly, "Just think! A doctor in the family. We're so proud of you, baby. Aren't we, Billy?"

"Of course! If that's what she wants. Everyone deserves to have what they want, if they work hard enough for it. Sure, if you work hard for something, and you want it bad enough, then you probably will get it." Billy said.

Louanne said, "It won't be easy. Pre-med and years of study beyond that . . . . and leaving home, too. That won't be easy."

Aunt Esther said, "Well, your Aunt Mabel . . . (with sarcasm), my beloved sister, made herself a happy life away from here. She certainly didn't lose any time leaving here, leaving all of us. She didn't seem to have any problem, I mean like missing us. So, I guess you can do it, too. You're smart like she was. She got out while the 'gettin' was good', before the old folk started getting sick and dying. I didn't have a chance. No big-city life with parties and high-flown friends all around you everywhere you go, no, not here for me. Nothing for me but hospitals and graveyards."

"Billy, I hope you have the good sense to at least finish high school. A drop-out is a loser. Nothing more than a loser, and that's all _he'll_ ever be." Calvin Jackson said, with his frown of disappointment in his son, Joe. It was dark on the front porch. No one could see the tear that ran down his hardened face.

After two weeks in classes, Louanne knew that she would flunk out before the end of the year. Her constant stress over the idea of becoming a doctor, a career which she had known for a few years that she did not really want, so pre-occupied her time that there was no concentration on her required courses of study. During the third week in college, she dropped all classes, giving up her scholarships. For the rest of the semester, she worked as a receptionist for a plastic surgeon. Frequently she called her father to tell him that all was going well and that she enjoyed college life.

Louanne, like her twin brother, was not especially good looking. She was seldom asked out on dates, and she had always been one of the first to be eliminated from the high school beauty contests, which her mother had always won. The trophy for "Miss Congeniality" was the only ones she was ever awarded. It was no stroke of luck that she found her receptionist job for the plastic surgeon's office. She had searched diligently for just such a job. Her nose needed fixing and her eye brows raised. The rest of the transformation she did on her own by starving off thirty pounds and working out regularly at an expensive gym. That is where most of her money went. She was hardly able to pay for the nose job, her rent, utilities and bits of health foods. But she was determined to change her appearance. Modeling lessons would come as early as she could find the money. She found a cheaper apartment. Less food was bought, bringing off the unwanted pounds and saving money at the same time.

Her determination increased when the modeling school's director told her she could never make it in the business "with a nose like that."

"But you do think that my body is right?" Louanne asked.

"You have a model's body, dear no boobs, no waist, cute ass, and five feet, ten inches of lean, flawless skin over good bone structure. But that nose . . . ."

A second job paid for the modeling lessons: the hair flipping, the attitude look, the moves that gave her body look like a willow branch blowing in a gently breeze, and a half-smile that was a combination of flirt, bitch and tease.

There was no time for a third job to pay for the nose fix. But she would find a way to get it done.

CALVIN

Calvin Jackson had married Lilly Mae Simples, the middle one of the Simples girls . . . the pretty one. After her death, Calvin was left with three small children. His sister-in-law was the only person to whom he could turn for help. She was the only one who had room for Calvin and his three children. The house had four bedrooms upstairs and two downstairs. There was a formal living room, a well-kept dining room (it was the most charming room in the house), with lovely, albeit faded, wall paper, and a very old, often polished dining room set. There was a crystal chandelier above the long table. It was the only one in the house. Table lamps lighted dark corners of the other rooms in the house. Calvin could afford to offer very little toward the upkeep of the house. Aunt Esther paid from her inheritance when there were repairs to be done. The leak in the upstairs hallway would have to wait until later. It had been leaking for several years. Although Mabel owned half of the house, she offered nothing towards its upkeep. After all, she had not lived there since she was nineteen years old. The outside walls of the house had not had a coat of paint in forty years. It was not likely to get one for many years, if ever again. Down the street three blocks was the First Baptist Church and the cemetery where Esther had "put away" many relatives, including her sister, her parents and her grandparents. Esther had resented her sister dying and leaving a baby and twins for her to raise. But a bond had taken place through the years. She also resented Mabel for leaving her to have to deal with sicknesses and eventual deaths. Calvin always expressed his appreciation, and offered as much money toward his children's needs as he could give. Most of the money went for food and clothing.

Although Calvin took an active part in raising his children when they were little, he spent less and less time at home as they grew older. Lottie Littlejohn required much of his time. Long before his wife had died, Calvin had started seeing Lottie. She thought that after Lilly had died and a decent amount of time had passed, that he would ask her to marry him. He did not. He knew, however, that there would be talk about it at some time. He hoped that the time would be far into the future. He liked the relationship just the way it was. He was with her only when he wanted to be with her, and she was always waiting for him.

MABEL

Mabel Katherine Sanders never married. She preferred the name "Sanders" over "Simples", and so she assumed Marvin Sanders last name. She never told anyone that Marvin had taken her in, had given her a bedroom and had fed her after her money had run out. She had not been evicted from her apartment in New York, but she had known that the time was near, since her waitress salary did not cover her living expenses. She had not even been able to arrange for a single audition. She had eventually become discouraged in her pursuit of becoming a successful actress, having met many young women whose talents were more refined, and whose beauty caught the attention of men and women in show business. She realized that she possessed neither of these sought-after qualities and therefore could not compete. She had never given up the idea of becoming an actress, even *being* one. She thought of herself as an actress and in a way, she actually became one. That is, she had a talent for making new acquaintances *believe* that she was an actress.

During her first years in New York, Marvin had really tried to help her win auditions. Being rather well-off, he even tried to buy her parts in small productions. He really cared for her and admired her ambitions to become an actress, a singer and/or dancer. He had paid for acting, voice and dance lessons. He actually knew a few people, ones who would give her the occasional walk-on, or one-liner parts on stage. She had not been the high school beauty queen, like her sister, Lilly, but as she aged a bit, her appearance took on a quality that would have given her success as a "character actress" had she acquired it in earlier years. Then, of course, there was the problem of too little real talent, which acting lessons failed to develop.

Marvin, after forty-five years of loving Mabel, died. He had been a rather unattractive, stout man who was considerably older than Mabel. Her love for him was something that Mabel never dared to question in her own heart. He was simply a necessity for her, a very important part of her life in New York. If she ever thought of how she felt about loving him, she would just ask the simple question, "How could I not love him." After his death, her thoughts would be, "I wish I had loved him more." After all, he had left to her his apartment, half a million dollars and, to her surprise, several small businesses, including a small cafe in a little known, noisy street in New York. Marvin had been good to her, having accompanied her to Alabama for weddings and funerals of a number of relatives and friends. No one from back home had gone to New York to his funeral. She had not notified them of his death until a few months after he had departed this world.

Mabel had never denied that she was in show business, as her sister, Esther, had not told everyone, nor did she reveal that Marvin was never her husband. She amazed herself at how quickly she became a business woman after his death. She was pleased with the management of the small businesses, trusting the people who had been Marvin's managers for years. Marvin's attorney had assured her that her businesses were doing well under the loyal people that Marvin had trusted. So, she left the businesses under the management which had served Marvin so well. Mabel, however, had insisted on running the small cafe, keeping the present manager on as her assistant with no reduction in his salary. Her reason for keeping the cafe was for her to realize her dream of becoming an entertainer. She had installed a small stage, with a burgundy velvet stage curtain, where she could perform. Sometimes she would sing a couple of songs in an evening, or do a dramatic reading, often to no more than eight or ten people. Still, she was the star of the show.

BILLY

Billy. There was always Billy . . . . what to do about him? What to do about Billy was a question which homesteaded in the back of everyone's minds (his father's, his Aunt Esther's, his teachers'). He was just there . . . . always, never asking, never demanding, and, apparently, never even wanting anything. But always there!

Calvin's silent observations of Billy through the last seventeen years had convinced him that his son had not the intelligence to go to college, not even to the two-year community technical school where he might learn a trade.

Upon approaching his eighteenth birthday, and high-school graduation, Calvin still had not heard Billy express interest in making any future plans. It was not that he had not tried to discuss Billy's future, indeed he had tried to pressure him into talking about some possible options. Billy would just remark, "I don't know." And he really did not know, as far as anyone could tell. Calvin's own plans for himself occupied much of his time, and troubled his mind in a worrisome way. That was because he could not settle in on what exactly he could plan for himself after Billy left home. He wanted Lottie for sure, but he was not so sure that he wanted to marry her. After Esther had helped him raise his children through all these years, he could not just leave her alone in her old age. Still he was not sure that it would be comfortable . . . . just his sister-in-law and he living alone together. He certainly could not ask Lottie to move in with him in Esther's house. Neither Esther nor Lottie would ever agree to that arrangement. They had never liked each other. Esther, for the most part hardly ever mentioned Lottie's name, nor did she make any remarks when anyone else did. Lottie spoke of Esther to Calvin, only when her jealousy would get the best of her. She resented the times when Esther's need for Calvin to be with the children for one reason or another would come before plans which Calvin and she might have made. Calvin could not move in with Lottie and leave Billy (with no apparent plans) for whom Esther would have to be responsible.

At times, it seemed that Billy was not capable of taking care of himself. Calvin could not depend on him to stay with Aunt Esther and assist her with problems to be brought on by her aging years.

"I saw a man down at Lottie's place last night." Billy said in his usual soft, quiet voice, almost as though he had not really said the words, but had just thought them aloud.

"Last night _when?_" Calvin demanded. Billy did not answer his father. He reached for the bowl of black-eye peas. Aunt Esther, across the dinner table from him, pushed the bowl closer. She said, "He went to a movie last night."

"What were you doing out last night? I thought you stayed at home to study for your exams." Calvin did not really want a discussion with Billy (he never did), but he was curious about the man Billy had seen at Lottie's place. He put his knife and fork down on the table beside his emptied plate, and looked at Billy, waiting for an answer. "What time last night?" Calvin asked.

"Didn't want to study. Didn't want to go to bed early, so I went downtown to the movie." Billy said, spooning out peas onto his plate. He broke off a piece of corn bread which Esther had baked.

"Boy, would you talk with some sense. What did you see? _Who_ did you see at Lottie's?" Calvin insisted on hearing answers.

"Don't know. Don't know who he was. I just saw him leaving her door as I ran by her house on my way home." Billy responded.

"What time was it?"

"'Bout midnight. Drove a black Hyundai".

Calvin's face was burning and his heart pounded too hard and too fast. It was the same sensation he had felt recently when Lottie and he had argued about the odor of cigarette smoke in her bedroom. Lottie did not smoke, and neither did he. This time the pounding heart concerned him, because it was accompanied by difficulty in breathing. He made an effort to calm himself. He did not want Esther and Billy to see him so upset by this news.

"Don't surprise me none." Esther said with conviction. Calvin glared at her, slowly pushed his chair from the table, turned to Billy with a questioning stare. Realizing that there would be no further answers, he left the room. Calvin took two aspirins and a sleeping pill and went to bed. Lottie would just have to wait.

The following evening when the telephone rang, Billy answered the call. "He's already gone to bed, Miss Lottie. No, I don't think he forgot last night. He just didn't feel well. And he don't feel good tonight either, so he went off to bed early again tonight. Sure, I'll tell him. Bye."

Esther had finished in the kitchen and came into the parlor. "Guess that was _her_."

"Yes'm. She was expecting him to come last night and again tonight, too."

"No matter." Esther said. "One's as good as another. That Lottie won't be lonely."

"You think Miss Lottie is lying about wanting to marry dad, Aunt Esther?" Billy asked.

Aunt Esther wanted to say, "You stupid dunce!" Instead she said, "Life is nothing but a bunch of promises . . . . and lies." They sat quietly for awhile before Esther asked, "Billy have you ever given a single thought to what you want out of your life?"

"I don't want anything. I just want to count for something. I mean I want my life to count for something. If it don't, I might just as well not live it."

Esther took a good, long look at his face as she tried to figure out his remark. She could not remember noticing what a handsome face it had become. Just a very handsome face, expressing nothing, revealing nothing. There was not a trace of the tell-all expressions which she used to see on Joe's face. And, unlike his sister, Billy had a nice, straight nose that tilted slightly upward near the tip. It occurred to her for the first time that he got his looks from his mother, who had been beautiful. The "pretty one". Why had she not seen his extreme good looks before? There he sat before her like a beautiful still-life picture in a frame. That was it. The frame. The picture was deserving of a better frame. The frame-work, his surroundings, did not do him justice. Perhaps he was not a masterpiece worthy of exhibiting in a royal palace, but certainly he should be in the presence of Hollywood stars, or among the wealthy, beautiful people who live lives of luxury in great mansions. But here he sat with his hint of a Mona Lisa smile (not really a smile, just a hint of a smile) in this shabby frame-work called Columbiana, Alabama. Alabama The Beautiful. And it was beautiful to her. It was where she belonged. But it was not where God should have dropped him on this big, green earth. Yet, he seemed to be content. At least he never complained about his existence. Not until now, when he offered the clue that he just wanted his life to count for something. Esther thought about her own life. She had never complained either, but she was far from content. She thought that most likely she never would be content, because she had never had a life of her own, and if she had ever had hopes and dreams, she could not remember what they were.

Billy did not have dreams. He had goals, plans which he had never shared with anyone. He did not know that anyone cared. It seemed to him that those close to him just did not know he was there most of the time. They knew his presence, but not his existence. He thought perhaps he could just walk away down the street, or down a country road and, like it was with Joe's leaving, they would soon forget that he had ever been there. Like Joe, he would go someday, but with a purpose other than just that of getting away.

JOSEPH, CARLOS AND ROSEANNE

In a small town somewhere between Nashville and Jackson, Mississippi, Joe and Carlos were caught in a thunderstorm. They found it necessary to find a dry place to spend the night. Several young people gathered on the front porch of an old abandoned house on a back street. The two boys walked up the steps to the high porch and found a spot where the roof was not leaking. Most of the young men and women, eight or ten, seemed to know each other. They were friendly enough to Joe and Carlos. One of the boys even offered Carlos a smoke. Joe watched as Carlos and the other boy talked and laughed together. He was relieved when a thin girl with long dark hair took Carlos' interest away from the boy. Joe knew that Carlos would have little interest in her. Joe tried to get some sleep, as did the others, as it was late.

The next day was sunny and warmer. Joe, Carlos and Roseanne, the dark haired girl Carlos had met the night before, hitch-hiked rides on into Jackson. They found Jackson to be very cosmopolitan. However, they also found a few sleazy places where they could earn a few dollars, enough to get by on until they moved on again. Roseanne could sing a little also, and she knew most of their songs. Joe did not like her. She always stood too close to Carlos, and it was not easy for Joe and Carlos to find time to be alone.

Eventually, Joe talked Carlos in to moving on toward New Orleans. He hoped that Roseanne would want to stay in Jackson, but she did not. She said that she had friends in New Orleans, and that she could find them a place to hang out until they made money to get their own place.

Once they were in New Orleans, Roseanne had difficulty locating her friends. She searched around the old hang-outs she used to know; sure that she would find them soon. Joe was busy trying to locate bars where they could get some gigs. It was not promising. New Orleans was not a country music town. He was successful, however, in losing Roseanne. He tricked Carlos into leaving the place where the three would usually meet on Magazine Street, by telling him that he had gotten them a job near Lake Pontchartrain, far across town. Joe insisted that the two of them go on alone.

"You can come back and find Roseanne later, maybe even tomorrow, but we need this job!"

"But she might think we've moved on and left her behind." Carlos said.

"Who cares what she thinks? She's not our problem. We're a team, you and me. We belong together. We don't need her." Joe insisted. Carlos was not happy about leaving her behind, but, as usual, he did not argue with Joe.

Soon they were working again. They were making a little money in a club that was noisy enough that no one could hear how bad their singing and picking was. Most of the regulars were drunk enough by the time they were on the little stage area, that they did not care how bad they were. The earnings were not good, but they could pay for a bedroom.

Sometimes, Joe would wake up and find Carlos gone. He knew that he was out trying to find Roseanne.

A few weeks passed, and they still had not been fired from the club. One evening as Joe was getting ready to go to the club, he was becoming concerned because Carlos had been gone most of the day. He came in just in time to leave with Joe to do their bit at the club.

"I guess I know where you've been all day. Why don't you just give up, Carlos? Roseanne has probably left New Orleans already.

You know how she was always talking about Atlanta and Destin. You're never going to find her!" Joe said.

Carlos replied, "I did." Joe did not try to hide the fact that he was not happy with this news.

"Carlos, just leave her alone. We were happy without her. It can be just like it used to be, just you and me. You've got to just leave her alone. We'll go away someplace and forget about her."

"Joe, I can't. She's pregnant. She says the baby's mine." Carlos told him.

"You did it with her? Damn, Carlos."

"Yes. More than once. I kind of liked it. She did, too."

"But she was doing other guys, too. It's probably not even yours"

Carlos said, "It doesn't matter. I want the baby anyway. She doesn't, but I do, because I'll always wonder if it was mine."

Joe tried to reason with Carlos. He tried to make him understand that he was not prepared to be a father. He had no money, no home and no family to help him with a baby. For the first time ever, Joe could tell that Carlos was not going to listen to him. "It wouldn't be fair to the kid, Carlos. What kind of life could you give it?"

"At least I can give it life! If I don't take it, Roseanne is going to get an abortion. Don't try to talk me out of this, Joe!" Carlos was firm.

"OK. Just forget it right now. We'll talk about it later. We have a show to do. Let's go." Joe put his arms around Carlos to calm him. Carlos would tremble, and sometimes cry when he became upset. Joe could always make it better, whatever the problem.

Joe spent the next month looking for him, for the next morning when he woke up, Carlos was gone.

COMING BACK HOME

Upon Billy's graduation from high school, Esther planned a great party for him. No one was in complete shock that he had graduated, but some found it difficult to hide their surprise. Actually, most of the family had not thought about it at all. Some distant relatives thought he was still in middle school, while others thought that he probably was a drop-out like Joe. Actually, Billy had been quite a good student, having fallen just a few points short of graduating with honors. None of them would ever know that. Neither Calvin nor Esther questioned him about grades, nor anything else concerning school, social life, friends, nor any problems which he might wish to discuss. Their main concern was about what he would do after graduation.

Billy was happy that Joe came home for his graduation. He did not. Joe's running out of money and luck just happened to coincide Billy's graduation. Joe had no where to go but back home. He was happy to see his family again, but not as happy as he would be to leave them again. He had not really had a happy day since Carlos skipped out on him. He did not expect, nor intend, to have another really happy day until he found Carlos again. They were a team, they could make it together in Nashville or New Orleans. They needed each other, no matter what Carlos was thinking when he slipped away during the night. Joe loved him. He would search for him until he found him, or spend the rest of his life trying.

There were laughter and smiles within the family as each one arrived. Joe and Billy drove to the airport in Birmingham to pick up Aunt Mabel. Louanne had her new boyfriend drive her home from Tuscaloosa, where the family thought she was still studying at The University of Alabama. Lottie Littlejohn had been invited by Calvin to join them for dinner. Esther had prepared a feast of a meal in Billy's honor. All his favorite foods, as well as favorites of some others were laid out on the elegantly decorated dining table, lighted with candles. Lottie had brought a pie, which Esther had deliberately left in the kitchen on the work table. When Lottie inquired of its whereabouts, Esther said, "We can have it later with coffee. If no one is still desiring of sweets after eating Billy's special chocolate cake, you can just take it back home with you."

Esther and Lottie had never liked each other and they usually were able to avoid each other's company. But tonight was special. Calvin's last child was now grown up and surely would be leaving home soon. Lottie would now have a chance to have Calvin all to herself. The family chatted conversations noisily across the table.

"Joe, where have you been so long?"

"Louanne's going to be a doctor, you know!"

"How are you getting on without Marvin? Was it sudden?"

"Just drifting here and there, picking up a gig now and then . . . nothing exciting."

"Calvin, will you be coming over later?"

"Maybe, I think Billy and Joseph are going out, so I'll leave the ladies here to visit together."

"How's your arthritis, Esther?"

"I told you before that it's diverticuler something, not arthritis. Mabel."

Later, Esther cleared away the dishes and put away food while Mabel sat and polished her nails.

"Marvin left everything to me. Actually, there was no one else to leave it to. He had no family. The apartment is small, only three bathrooms and four bedrooms. Not big like this house. I could sell one of the businesses and buy a larger one. There is some money, too. And the businesses are prosperous, and I don't have to be bothered with running them. Of course, I keep my eyes on the books. I know where every penny goes and exactly how much comes in each month. I eat my meals at my restaurant. It's small, but I have regular customers. I enjoy running the restaurant. I use some of mama's old recipes. Good Southern food is appreciated by many New Yorkers. And the restaurant does allow me to continue my show business career, even at my age."

Esther did not stop putting dishes away. She asked, casually, "How do you have time to keep up with all those businesses and that restaurant, and keep your acting career going at the same time? And whatever would you want with a bigger apartment? I hate this big old thing."

"Oh. Well, I don't get as many parts on stage as I used to. I manage." She hesitated a minute before she asked, "What do you mean, you hate this house? What is there to hate about our lovely old home place?"

"You could probably answer that for yourself if you had been stuck here like I was. But you escaped as early as you could." She turned to look at her sister, putting a bowl into the kitchen sink. "Or maybe you just had things figured out better than I did."'

Calvin, Louanne and Lottie sat in the parlor. Lottie, showing her impatience, said, "It's getting late, Calvin! If you are going to visit with me any tonight, we need to go on down to my house."

"I think I'll just stay here and talk with my beautiful daughter." Calvin said.

"Yes, she is beautiful, after having that awful hump taken off her nose. What else did you have done, honey?" Lottie asked.

"Nothing. Just a little nose job. And I lost a few pounds, too. Miss Lottie, a few nips and tucks would do wonders for you." Louanne said.

"You run along home, Lottie. I'll see you tomorrow. I want to spend the evening with my daughter. I want to hear all about her college experiences."

"Well, that could take awhile. Seems like it's taking her a long time to get that diploma or degree or *whatever* it is that she's getting." Lottie said, preparing to leave.

"I said I'll see you tomorrow, Lottie." Calvin repeated.

"So be it!" Lottie said, and smiled sweetly at both of them as she departed.

Calvin said, "So. Tell me all about it. Everything you're involved in. And I want to know about that boyfriend, too. Is this a serious relationship?

"The boyfriend . . . . not serious. College . . . . well . . . . it's a challenge, but I am enjoying my life." Louanne hoped there did not have to be much discussion. She did not like lying to her father.

"I'm so proud of you, Louanne. Joe . . . well, I'll never understand him. And Billy . . . . well, I don't even try to understand him. Strange boy, that Billy. Really, sometimes he seems just like a stranger here in the house." Calvin's gloomy look was noticed by Louanne.

"I hope you will not be disappointed in me, Dad, no matter what . . . . whatever happens, please don't be disappointed in me." The guilt of lying to her father, the pain she felt for not becoming what he had wanted her to be might have been seen in her face, had her father been looking at her. However, his gaze was downward at his shoes.

"Never!" He promised. "Well, I think I will go down the street and visit with Lottie for a bit. She seemed to be really upset with me for standing her up a few times lately."

"Sure, Dad. I understand. I'm rather tired anyway, so I think I'll turn in for the night. Or perhaps I will study for my final exams for awhile before I go to bed." She lied again.

Joseph and Billy went to a bar in Birmingham. It was Billy's first time ever to go into a bar, and he had had only one beer before. He had not liked it. Joseph like it, and he had too many. Too many beers always caused him to talk too much. He started telling Billy about Carlos and how much fun they had with Carlos singing and he playing the guitar.

"Where is your guitar? You didn't bring it home with you." Billy inquired.

"Oh. I had to hock it to by food on my way to Alabama." He had not intended to continue this line of conversation, but his tongue was under the control of an unspecified number of beers. "After Carlos left me, I was no good. I can't sing worth a damn by myself. And I missed him so much, I didn't want to sing nor play. I just wandered about kind of lost, then my money ran out and I found myself on my way back home."

"Where did Carlos go?" Billy asked, not really caring.

"I don't know. He left me in the middle of the night . . . . in the middle of nowhere. Somewhere near New Orleans." He downed a few more swigs of beer. "Damn him!"

They sat quietly for awhile. Billy was trying to figure out this picture. Where had Joseph met Carlos, what was their relationship? And why did he not just find another singing partner and keep moving on?

Joseph said, "If I didn't love him so much, I'd kill him when I find him!"

"What if you don't ever find him?"

"I'll find him. I _will_ find him somewhere, someday."

Calvin stopped near the corner of Lottie's yard fence that ran along the sidewalk. The little white house and its white picket fence shone brightly in the moonlight. It was easy to see that the man getting out of the little black Hyundai was John Morrison. Calvin did not feel like a fight, and he did not want to face Lottie with this problem tonight.

THEIR DREAMS (ESTHER AND MABEL)

Summer vacation was not a time to which Esther was looking forward, at least not with any excitement. Calvin and his three children and Mabel, all to cook for, and worse of all, she would have to be listening to their never-ending babble concerning topics about which had not the slightest bit of interest. She especially had a dread for Mabel's constant chatter about her past experiences and future plans in New York. Future plans. What would it be like to have future plans, Esther wondered. All of her life, her only plans were to get everything taken care of day by day.

Billy had graduated only a few weeks earlier, and Joseph had left with a couple of friends, two other drop-outs, he had known back in his school days. He was back in a few weeks, looking thinner and weary. Louanne was coming home just long enough to level with her family about her not being in medical school. She was driving a new car, her own. Billy met Mabel at the airport.

After the second night of everyone's arrival, and the second evening meal which she had prepared for the six of them, Esther found herself clearing off the dining room table without help again. Mabel sat at the breakfast table in the kitchen, making an effort to show Esther pictures she had made at Niagara Falls recently. Esther glance at them briefly as she passed by with dirty dishes. She was taken by surprise when Mabel suddenly announced, "Esther, I have decided to stay here. All the kids will be leaving soon, out on their own. And I expect Calvin will marry, or at least move in with that Littlejohn woman, after they have all gone. You don't need to be here all alone in this big old house."

"But what about your businesses. Don't you need to be in New York to see to all that?" Esther said, alarmed by this news. She could not imagine a life with Mabel around constantly.

"I want you to make a life for yourself, now. I can help you keep up the house, and you can use your money to travel some. Maybe meet a man . . . ."

"Mabel, what's your problem? You've never been concerned about me before. Don't pretend to be now! What's your real reason for this sudden decision?" Esther sat across the table from Mabel, and waited for her answer.

"Why, Esther Simples, I've not made a *sudden* decision. I've always been concerned about you, with the dreadful situation Lilly's death left you in."

Esther was silent for a moment before she decided she would say, "You mean you were concerned about Lilly's death and your lack of interest in helping to share the load.

Lilly, mama, papa, cousins, uncles, aunts . . . . all the funerals, the arrangements.

Three children for me to raise and Calvin . . . . A family to care for that was not mine!

Meals to prepare, school work to help with, teachers to meet with, clothes to wash and iron . . . . Calvin's white shirts to keep clean and pressed so he could go courting Lottie Littlejohn!" Esther looked around her kitchen for a minute. Tears came to her eyes. They were tears that she did not want Mabel to see. But what did it matter if Mabel saw her tears? She turned back to look at her sister. "And all the time, Lottie was seeing John Morrison, too!" Esther wiped away a tear before it rolled down her aging cheek.

"Well, you didn't *try* to get him, Esther. You just let Lottie take John Morrison away from you." Mabel replied. "And the man did kind of like you."

"I didn't have time to go gallivanting around. I had people to take care of. You don't know how it was. You were living it up in New York City! You had your celebrity life in New York City on the stage. I couldn't even make the time to come to see even one of your performances, and I really wanted to see my sister on the stage. I wanted to come back home from New York City and brag about my successful sister!" Esther said it with restraint and reluctance.

There was a silence before Mabel said, in a low and sorrowful voice, "There was no stage career. I was never a celebrity. I never made it as an actress. I wasn't good enough. If it had not been for Marvin, I would have had to come back home . . . . or starve to death. I've pretended to be something I'm not all these years. At this age, it is not any fun pretending anymore."

"So it was all just a lie? And what about Marvin's money and businesses? Was that a lie, too? And the restaurant? Just another lie? So, now you have nothing. That's the only reason you want to come back home after all these years." Esther accused.

Mabel answered, "No, I have the businesses, some money . . . . in fact, I'm quite well-off. And the restaurant is for real. It's mine. I can perform on my small stage anytime I want to, whether there is an audience or not. Esther, I really wanted to come back here to do something for you. I couldn't stand to come back here when there was so much sickness and death. That's all anyone ever talked about . . . . whatever part of the anatomy hurt, and who hurt the most . . . . and who would probably be the next to go. I just didn't want to hear it. And with Lilly's three fussy children . . . . well, Columbiana was just not my cup of tea. New York was fun! Alive! Even without success in the theatre, Marvin always provided me with a good time . . . . when he was still alive."

"Then go back to it. Go after that dream of the theatre." Esther said. Mabel thought that she was being unkind at first, then she realized that her sister was serious. Esther continued, "If I had a dream, I'd never give up on it until I realized that dream . . . or until I die."

"Well, I couldn't achieve mine, so I eventually gave up. Enough wasted years I spent trying."

"You can still have it, Mabel. Even if you can't act, you probably can direct. Move your tables around to the walls of the restaurant, put a small stage in the middle, and start a dinner theatre. You could help lots of young hopefuls get started in their acting careers. If you discovered just *one,* wouldn't that make *you* a success?" She was getting Mabel's attention. She had to. There was no way she was going to have Mabel live there with her.

Mabel looked at her sister with amazement. Why had she herself not thought of that? Such a simple little solution toward living her dream, and it was her sheltered, boring sister, who had never been out of the state of Alabama, who had solved her problem. Indeed, she had changed her outlook for the future. Suddenly, Mabel did not feel as old as she did yesterday. Suddenly, Esther was greatly relieved.

THEIR DREAMS (JOSEPH AND LOUANNE)

The pear tree had a few dead branches and other signs of its old age, broken branches, knotted bark and a large decayed area revealing hollowness in the trunk. Yet, life was still running through the branches, as the tree was always aglow in the springtime with its white blossoms, promising another abundant crop of pears. That was the way it had been last May when Louanne was at home for Billy's graduation. Now, as she and Joseph sat under the tree, there were half-grown green pears that pulled the branches low with their weight. Joseph snapped off a small twig with several green pears. He sniffed of the little pears, ever searching for the sweet smell of life. A scent which he had seldom smelled, and not at all since he had lost contact with Carlos.

"Joe, I need to tell you something." Louanne started. "Actually, I need to tell Dad, but I'm afraid he will be terribly upset with me, and very disappointed as well."

"If this is about your not studying pre-med, you don't have to worry. He already knows." Joseph said, matter-of-factly.

"He *knows? You know?* " She was surprised.

"It was one of those situations which usually does not happen in real life." He said.

"I had no place to go, and no money when I hitched a ride back in to Birmingham. I decided to look you up at The University of Alabama, and maybe get a few bucks from you to get on home. As

I was leaving the Administration Building, I ran face-to-face into Dad. I think he was suspicious of what you were doing, but he said he was just coming to give you a surprise visit. I told him not to waste his time, because I had just been told that you dropped out of college long ago, after only a few weeks."

"What did Dad say? Was he angry, hurt, worried?" Louanne asked.

"He was more worried than anything. He had to find out where you were and what you were doing. But his biggest concern was that you had not told him." Joseph said. "You know that you are the one he could always count on, and he was hurt that you did not tell him."

"That was a big concern for me, too, but I didn't know what his reaction would be." Louanne said.

They started their walk from the orchard back to the house. Joseph said, "He wants us to be happy, I guess. And I think he just wants to be free from the feeling that it is his responsibility to make us happy. I suppose he cannot have a life of his own, maybe with Lottie, until he feels rid of that responsibility to us."

"Aunt Esther has been the one to take care of us. Dad has always had a life of sorts with Lottie." Louanne's resentment of Lottie was not small.

"Sure he has, but soon he can leave Aunt Esther's house and be free of her rules. I certainly understand that. And don't forget that Dad worked hard to have money when we needed anything." Joseph reminded her that event though Calvin spent a lot of time with Lottie, it was their father who had supported them financially. Sure, he appreciated the home life which Aunt Esther had given them, but it was hardly the home life which his father had wanted.

"Does he know what I am doing, I mean instead of going to college?

"It was easy enough to find out. That was by coincident, too. Dad took me to a restaurant downtown Tuscaloosa, near the campus. Close to the restaurant was a photographer's shop. In the window was a big picture of you. You looked different, prettier, but we knew right off that it was you. We went inside and the photographer told us all about you. He said that you were an 'up-and-coming new model.'. Dad called the modeling agency to verify what we'd been told. He was relieved to know that you were doing all right. We ate, and then I came on back home with him. I had no other choice, and, besides, he asked me to. He told me not to let you know what we had learned. He's just waiting for you to tell him. He knows you will. You should, right away."

Louanne said, "I will. Soon. I'll tell him before I leave tomorrow." As they neared the house, Louanne sat down on a stone bench under the shade of thousands of leaves of an old willow oak.

"Well, it's my dream. To be a model." Her twin sat down beside her. "What about you, Joe? Do you have any dreams? I hope you have at least some *plans* which will take you away from here.?"

He chose his words carefully. "Yes, I have *one*. To find him. And someday I will." Louanne knew her twin brother better than anyone else. She knew that he had said all that he intended to say. And she knew that he had not said it to her, but to himself. And she was glad that he had said it not to her.

THEIR DREAMS (BILLY AND CALVIN)

Billy checked the grocery items off the list as his father found each of them on the grocery store shelves. Esther had included on the list a frozen cake and a gallon of ice cream. She had not the time to bake more cakes to satisfy this sweet-toothed Southern family. She was tired of baking, and she was tired of family and their friends who dropped in unexpectedly to visit with them.

"So, what is next, Billy?" Calvin asked.

"Ground beef, for meat loaf, I suspect."

"No, son. I mean what is next for you, in your life. What do you want to do? I think I can put you through college, if you think you can make it, or at least through technical for two years." Calvin waited for an answer, but none came. He continued to make suggestions, determined to move the matter forward. "Or you could probably find a job in Birmingham, get your own apartment and have a little fun before you make any serious decisions. If you want to travel a little, I could send you to Europe for a few weeks, maybe to Paris or London. I've been able to save a little money, not having to pay Louanne's expenses. And Joe well, he doesn't seem to need anything I have to offer including advice." Still no thoughts on the subject appeared to show in Billy's behavior. He just continued to call out the names of items from the grocery list.

"The important thing, Billy, is that you do concentrate on making some decisions about your future. It's not good for young people not to prepare themselves for something." His father insisted.

"I've already made a decision. I've been concentrating on it for awhile. I'm going to join the armed services. I'm going to Iraq." He said it so casually that it almost did not register with his father's worried mind, but with such conviction that when his father did grasp what he had said, he was stunned, shocked to a degree that caused him to drop a can of green beans which he had just taken from a sale display.

"Whoa!" The two looked each other eye-to-eye, maybe even for two minutes. Calvin could not stop looking into his son's eyes. He concentrated on those blue eyes that seemed to sparkle for the first time ever. At least Calvin had never seen the sparkle in them. What Billy had just announced to him was still ringing in his ears, but he was entranced by his son's eyes. "By God! Your eyes are just the same as your mother's were! She had the prettiest blue eyes ever. Funny how I never noticed that you have her eyes."

"Am I like her, really?"

"No. Not really _like_ her. She was more out-going than you. She smiled more." Calvin said, still gazing into his son's eyes. Calvin felt tears forming around his eyelids. "But you are more like her than the twins. I mean, you look more like her."

The father and son finished their shopping and left the store. In the car, Calvin said, "She would have been proud of what you just told me back there in the store. I am too. But we need to discuss this before you make such a _serious_ commitment. We need to talk about that decision, Billy."

"I've already made that decision. I'm going to help defend my country." Billy declared.

Calvin could not stop the tear that rolled down to become lost in his mustache. He did not know if the tear was from how proud he was of his son at that moment, or from the sudden fear he had that his son might die in Iraq. He was driving slowly. He wanted time to think and time to talk to his son. "People are getting killed over there, Billy. Every day. Our people, our sons are dying over there, and even though we know they are defending our country, some of us don't even know . . . . from what?

"I know. I understand that. I watch the news on TV. I'm not sure if we should be there, but we are. I'm not better than any one of them. And I don't mean just Americans, but Iraqis, too. If I have to give up my life to save just one of them . . . . well, maybe that's why I'm here on God's green earth. And if I do just one good deed, save just one life, help just one person to live in a free country, then I will have the answer to 'why am I here?'" This time Billy saw the tear that slid down his father's face. He said no more. Neither father nor son said more. There was no need for anything else to be said, because that one tear had said it all.

THEIR DREAMS (MABEL AND JOSEPH)

"No one told me! Well, I heard that you play the guitar, but I had no idea that you are in show business! Joe, I am so happy for you." He was driving Aunt Mabel to the airport in Birmingham. She was returning to New York to set up her dinner theatre.

"Well, I'm not really in 'show business', not like you, Aunt Mabel. We barely made a living. Sometimes we didn't. _Many times_ we didn't! Those times, I really wanted some of Aunt Esther's grits."

"I suppose that you will go back on the road again soon?" Mabel asked, applying another coat of very red lipstick.

"Yes, soon." He said. And he was thinking, "not on the road to perform, but to find Carlos, wherever he may be."

"Oh! I have a great idea." Mabel suggested, "If you are ever in New York, you could do a . . . uh . . . what's it called? A gag or . . . ."

"In our case, we probably should be gagged, but, no, it's called a 'gig'". Joseph laughed. "And that would be really great, to do a gig in New York."

"You could be the entertainment while my customers are finishing their dinners, before the play begins. Who knows, it could go on for years!" Mabel's excitement caused Joseph to have a mental image of Carlos and he singing on a stage in New York.

"You can count on it, Aunt Mabel." But Joseph's own bit of excitement soon turned to despair. He had no idea where Carlos might be, nor how long it could take for him to ever find his friend. He would begin his search where he last saw him, somewhere near New Orleans, Louisiana.

THEIR DREAMS
(LOUANNE, BILLY AND ESTHER)

"Why, Billy? Why would you put yourself in such a dangerous situation? You're too young to . . . ." He interrupted Louanne and finished her sentence, "To die? Louanne, no one is too young, nor too old, to die. And everyone should make some effort, in their own way, to make life better for other people. This is my way."

"That's an admirable thought, Billy. But death is permanent. And you could die in Iraq."

"I know that, but I could come back unharmed. If I don't, well, like everyone else should be able to do, I will have done what I wanted to do in life. I'm thinking of my life, not my death." Billy looked at his beautiful sister. He said, "Louanne, you want to become a model. Work hard at becoming one. Enjoy life and follow your own dream. That's what I will be doing, following my dream, doing what I think is right for me."

Aunt Esther entered the kitchen and sat with them. "I'm glad somebody has a dream."

Louanne poured her aunt a glass of milk. "Aunt Esther, you will soon be in this big old house alone. Will you miss us, all of us and all of our noise?"

"Maybe. Sometimes I've felt pretty lonely even with everyone here. Right now . . . . I'm just tired."

"I know you are tired of cooking for the family, tired of housework, and probably tired of all our noise. You need some rest, some peace and quiet for a change." Billy said.

Louanne suggested, "Aunt Esther, why don't you sell this old house and move into one of those assisted living places? You could make friends with people your age, maybe you could even find yourself a man."

"Why does everybody think I need a man? I don't, not at my age. He would just be someone else to have to take care of, and finally bury." But Esther's thoughts did turn to John Morrison. She thought, "Too late." And after all, she did not want him now, not after he had been with Lottie Littlejohn. "No man for me, thank you. I'll manage well by myself. And friends, I have learned, will only cause you to waste your time listening to their problems." Then she turned to Billy. "When are you leaving, Billy?"

"In a couple of weeks. I'll be in basic for a few weeks before I go to Iraq." The three of them sat quietly and drank their milk with Aunt Esther's tea cakes, made from an old family recipe which had come with their ancestors from England. The British would have called them biscuits. But here in the South, a biscuit was something quite different. Esther suspected that this would be the last time she would have anyone with whom to share her tea cakes.

LOTTIE AND CALVIN

"You actually spied on me? Damn, Calvin, that's a pretty low-down thing to do after all we've shared together!" Lottie was angry, but she knew that she was the guilty one. She brought wine glasses and a bottle from the kitchen.

"More 'low-down' than you cheating on me, Lottie . . . 'after all we've shared together.'? Calvin showed his hurt in his face.

"Well, it's not like I belong to you. I've waited long enough for a proposal of marriage. A girl gets tired of waiting. I ain't getting any younger, and neither are you, Calvin." Lottie said. "Sit down and pour our wine."

Calvin sat on the sofa. Pouring the wine, he said, "I'm as young as John Morrison. Guess I can still do anything he can do. Can you deny that, Lottie?"

"Not when you are not here, Calvin! You can't do anything if you are not here to do it! And I've spent too many nights alone waiting for you to show up, lately." Lottie said.

"I'm sorry about that. But the children are gone now, even Billy." Then anger replaced his sadness and he said, "But it seems to me that you haven't spent many nights alone. I have found out that while I have been fulfilling obligations to my family, that, unbeknownst to me, you were not spending too many nights alone!"

"What are you suggesting, Calvin? That I've had all amounts of men in my bedroom?" Lottie's anger was growing, as well as her regret that Calvin knew about John Morrison's visits with her.

"No. What I'm saying is that if I'm not enough for you, then lucky for you that you have other friends, because I'm not willing to marry a woman that can't be true to me." Calvin said.

"I've been true to you, waiting for you, just for *you* for more than twenty years! I wanted you even before Lilly died. You know that! And I thought you wanted me, too. How long do I have to wait, Calvin?" She shouted.

"You don't have to wait. You have not been waiting, not for me. You've been waiting for John Morrison, and he can have you. I've been waiting, too, you know. Waiting for the right time for us. Now would have been the right time, and I found out that you've been seeing John, and God knows who else, for a long time." As he starts to leave, Lottie yells to him, "Don't you dare leave me tonight, Calvin Jackson! If you do, I swear I'll call John Morrison to come over here tonight. You can't walk out on me tonight, after all these years, without suffering consequences."

Calvin stopped at the door. He did not look back at Lottie. He did not want her to see the tears that seemed to come so easily in recent months. He said, "Maybe I'll be back . . . maybe I won't." He left.

Lottie poured wine to refill both the glasses. She drank them both during spells of crying and babbling angry phrases. Hurt, angry, humiliated, embarrassed and lonely, she drank the rest of the bottle. She cried aloud, as she staggered off to the kitchen for another bottle, "Damn you, Calvin Jackson! Damn you!"

JOSEPH AND CARLOS

"I told you we should have left yesterday!" Joseph yelled to Carlos, as he handed the baby through the window. They climbed the fire escape to its top level as wind, rain, water and debris, large pieces of buildings and signs swirled through the world around them. They reached the flat rooftop and stood knee-deep in water, five stories above the street level below. They held each other, the baby between them, wet, cold, and trembling with fear.

"Joe, you knew this hurricane was coming through New Orleans. Why did you come back here?" Carlos asked.

"This is no time to be stupid, Carlos! I came here to find you, because I love you! I would have come through hell as well as this high water to get to you.!" They had to yell to each other in order to be heard above the roar of the storm.

"Well, that's just what you did, because this water is hell! I don't think we're going to make it out of here, Joe. I'm scared!" Carlos was crying. They were holding on to each other and the baby in order not to be blown off one by one. If they went, they would all go together. Their eyes were burning with tears and muddy Mississippi River water mixed with the horrors of foreign matter.

"We've got to make it, Carlos. We have to get this baby to dry land."

Joseph waded to the edge of the roof-top. Just below was an empty boat floating toward them. "Carlos, come here! There's a boat. I've got to stop it." Joseph jumped several feet down into the boat. When he looked up, Carlos was wading along the edge of the roof-top holding the baby tightly.

"Drop him down to me. Hurry, the current is too strong for me. I have no way to stop the boat!" Carlos carefully aimed the baby toward Joseph's waiting arms. He let go. Joseph caught him.

"Hurry, Carlos, jump!" The boat was moving away from the building now, bumping into bodies and furniture. Carlos yelled, "If I don't make it, promise you'll take care of him, Joseph!"

"Just shut the fuck up and jump!" Joseph yelled.

After Carlos splashed into the dark, nasty water, he went under and never came back up to the surface.

As Joseph lay on his new, clean cot, he tried to remember how long he had looked back for Carlos. He did not know how he and the baby had been carried to the bus. He could not remember how many hours, nor days the ride was before he was admitted to a shelter for the Katrina hurricane victims. He must have eaten, because he was not hungry. He pulled the baby closer to him and kissed his rosy cheeks. Joseph whispered to the baby, "I love you, Carlos."

ESTHER AND CALVIN

Esther entered the parlor with the mail in one hand and a small bunch of violets in the other. "Seems too early for violets to be blooming." She said.

"Pretty. Violets were Lilly's favorite flower. You would think she would have liked lilies best, considering her name. But I'm sure it was violets." Calvin said.

"And mine, too. They smell so sweet, and they're mighty pretty." Esther said. "Speaking of pretty, look at your daughter. Our Louanne is real pretty." Calvin was shuffling through the pieces of mail. Esther continued, "She's on the back of that magazine, an advertisement for some hair product." Esther walked from the parlor on into the kitchen.

Calvin said, "Well, I'll be damned! It's her alright. She's finally realizing her dream. Good. That's what I want for her. Happiness. That's what happiness is, realizing your dreams coming true." He walked to the front door and looked down the street in the direction of Lottie's house. At first, after their quarrel, she had called every night. They would talk, but he never went to her. The calls had become less frequent. And, now, she never called at all. Sometimes, after dark he would walk passed her house, but he would not stop to visit with her, even if there was no strange car in her driveway.

*   *   *

Billy had been buried in the family plot at the First Baptist Church cemetery, near his mother. Calvin did not know how much of his son was in the casket. Louanne was in Paris. She would visit his grave when she returned. Her photo shoot in Paris was very important for her career. Mabel stayed on for a few days after the funeral. No one knew where Joseph was. At the funeral, Esther had stood beside her brother-in-law. "You can't fault him, Calvin. For joining, I mean. He wanted to go and do his part. He represented us, all of us, over there. I'm proud of him. He was my pick of the children, but I didn't know it until after he had left home."

Lottie stood in back of the few people who showed up for the hero's burial. She made her presence known, but never spoke words of consolation to Calvin. As soon as their eyes met, Lottie wiped tears from her eyes and walked back home.

Before Esther left, she said, "I'll go on home and start you some dinner. Mabel will be hungry, too." Calvin still did not speak. He stayed after everyone had gone except the men who were there to throw shovels of dirt over his son's remains.

CALVIN AND LOTTIE

Calvin had walked the short distance from the cemetery, passing Lottie's house slowly, on his way home. He even stopped for a few seconds in front of her house, contemplating whether to knock at her door. He decided to walk on to his own house. Then he thought, "It's not my house. I have no house. I don't even have a home anymore." Standing in front of the big house where his children had grown up, the house they had called "home", he just looked around the property, the house, the orchards, the vegetable garden, the tall, old trees. Suddenly, he felt that he could not stand even the thought of going back into the house. He did not want to see his two sisters-in-law, neither of which he knew had ever really liked him. And he did not like them, either.

Calvin got into his car and started out of town. All afternoon, he drove around the countryside on back, narrow highways and dirt roads. He was trying to figure it out. It was not possible to figure out a solution to a problem over which he had no control. He was not sure that he even knew, understood the problem. He felt the sadness, the grief, the sorrow, the disappointments, the failures, but still there was something else that would never allow him to know another day of happiness. What was he to do? Where was he to go? What did he want? Had he ever really wanted anything? He had not asked to be put on this earth. Even his marriage had followed a mistake. He had never asked for children. He had never asked for anything. Nothing. Nothing is what he had, now, and he had not even asked for that.

Later in the evening he stopped in front of Lottie's house. Without even thinking about it, he knocked at her door. He was let in. The house was different. It had been "let go", so to speak. Lottie obviously had not cleaned the house in days. Empty bottles lay around the coffee table and on the floor. Lottie was drunk.

"Well?" She asked.

"Well, I just I don't know. I don't know why I'm here." Calvin muttered.

"I know why you used to come, in days gone by. But why are you here now? What do you want, Mr. Calvin Jackson?" Lottie swayed and bumped her leg on the coffee table.

"What do I want? I don't know what I want, Lottie. Everybody, everything I ever had, I've lost. And I can't even feel that I miss whatever I had, that I am not even sure I ever wanted in the first place. My wife died years ago. My children Louanne, she's gone far away. I don't know where Joseph is. Billy was blown to Kingdom Come. The only place I have to lay my head is in an old house that belongs to two old maid sisters-in-law." He lifted his gaze up from the floor to Lottie's eyes. "And I guess that I lost what you and me had, if we ever had anything but a bed. I have nothing left."

"Neither do I. After all the hopes and dreams, all the years of waiting for you, I got nothing. I wanted to be your wife. But you turned me into what you see a lush and a whore that no one comes to see anymore!" Her speech was slurred from her drunkenness. "Even John Morrison met some young, *decent* broad in Birmingham, and married her."

"I'm sorry for that. For what I did, I mean. It just happened that way, didn't it?" Calvin just looked at her for a few more seconds and turned to walk to the door. He stopped to say to her, "I said that I never wanted anything. But now I do. I want to die. I just want to die, that's all. I wish I were dead."

Lottie put her bottle down on the couch and walked to a corner cabinet. She took something out of a drawer. Calvin saw, when she turned back to face him, that it was a pistol.

"You wish you were dead? Why not. I gave my life to you. You gave me nothing. But I can grant you your wish." It took only one bullet. Then, she turned the gun to her own heart.

ESTHER

Esther waved good-bye to Mabel and Louanne, as the taxi drove away. She sat on the front stoop for awhile listening to the birds in the tree tops. The sky was blue. She walked into the yard and plucked a few roses before going back into the house. Everyone was gone. The house was strangely empty of sounds. She could hear only the sound of clocks ticking the refrigerator motor humming. For the first time in her life, she was alone. She put the roses in a vase with water. She washed a couple of drops of blood from her finger, having been pricked by a rose thorn. She dried her hands with a paper towel, then walked back into the parlor and turned on the ceiling fan. Esther looked around the room. She walked to a window and looked out beyond the rose garden. She looked through the doors to other rooms. Aloud, she said, "What a nice, old house." She smiled, and said, "Funny . . . . how I never noticed that before."

Running Fast Before the Blade

By
Robert Bertrand

RUNNING FAST BEFORE THE BLADE

Breaking the "new ground" was not an easy chore. Trees had to be chopped down, and the stumps thereof had to be dug up. The tree trunks and branches were sawed, or chopped into fire-place or wood-stove length pieces, loaded on to the ground slide, since the wagon had a broken wheel, and pulled to the house (by mules). We spent days, even weeks during the cold of winter, clearing away trees, bushes and weeds, dead from the winter freezes. Rocks, small and large, had been carried to the edge of the cleared earth before springtime arrived. The only life left were the honeysuckle and trumpet vines, clinging to the fences in the March winds. Kudzu would begin to spread into the area from distant fields, if we did not squelch its rapid growth, not an easy task.

As the days turned from bitter cold to welcomed warmth of spring's promise, the ground no longer appeared to be "new ground". Instead, it was a barren field awaiting the cutter, which would eliminate most of the high grass and weeds. Following would be the plow, which would turn the small plot into a field, a field ready for the planting of corn, cotton, peanuts, or millet.

Papa was as proud of this sweet earth as I would have been of a new dress. I was only fourteen years old. I wore overalls and one of papa's shirts. I could never know if papa was happy as we labored throughout the long days, from sunup until sundown, until "quitting-time" when I could see in his eyes the pleasure he found in the accomplishments for which we were put on this acreage. He always said that it was God's soil, and that He put us in charge of taking care of it. I could never quite see it from his point of view. I figured if it was God's possession, then what business did we have to be cropping out the natural growth which He had let be there.

But what did I know of God's business, and what did I know of a farmer's views on such things.

The ground looked prettier and prettier everyday. Papa was so proud, and when he plowed through the soil for the first time, I stood near the outcropping under a big, old water oak and watched him urge the mule forward through the undisturbed soil, where small roots and rocks still made for difficult plowing. The roots would soon decay, but the rocks would be wheel-barrowed to the edge of the field, by myself, where they would form a borderline along the edge of the field. They would also offer some refuge for the crawling, hopping and running creatures which had fled from the axes, saws, blades and plows that were destroying their habitat for generations untold.

Watching papa was like watching an artist at work, making something beautiful. I could envision how the field would look in midsummer, with tall, green corn swaying in the summer breezes, ears of green corn with golden-yellow silk flowing from the tender shucks that covered and protected the baby grains of corn. I had a mental image of late summer cotton, snow-white with browning leaves glistening with early morning dew. In my mind's eye, I could see tall stacks of peanut-vine hay against the distant sunset of early fall.

There were other visions which seized an underlying emotion. It would sometimes surface itself by choking me, making it hard for me to breathe even the freshest country air. It was during those times that I would have a sad feeling, almost a feeling of grief come over me like a sudden storm which would sweep away everything in its path. It was a sorrowful feeling which I did not understand. I would stand and look across the newly plowed rows in the field, all the way to the farther edge near the woods where I saw wild turkeys lurking about as though they were in a daze, wondering what had happened to their territory, their homes, their nests. At sight of me, they would slowly ease into hiding into the underbrush of the woods. Sometimes, they would take to the air and disappear through the tree tops. Occasionally, a deer would wander onto its former grazing area. I could see a rabbit, and he could see me. I wondered if he would run. He was wondering if he should. Looking along the edge of the new field, I saw other small animals, chipmunks, field mice, possums, gazing on the field, then quickly moving back into the brush, or into the piles of rock where some had already established new homes.

Birds of many feathers flew overhead, but none stopped as they used to when there were trees and wild blueberry bushes. They no longer lingered to chirp, nor screech at our invasion of their homeland.

I began to wonder whether what was progress and beautiful reward for hard work for us was devastation for the ones whose homes, playgrounds, and livelihoods we had destroyed. I wondered if we had taken care of His land in the way that God intended for us to do. Papa did not seem to even question such a thought, and somehow, at that moment, I loved him less. I loved myself less, too. But that is just the way papa was. He had no patience with people who did not like to work, just as he did not like to see land lying unused. He did not care for trees, nor bushes that did not produce something to eat or to sell. Sooner or later such useless growth would get the ax, regardless of its graceful shape, its delightfully scented blossoms, or the cooling shade it would offer in the hot days of summer.

When I would become tired and wish for rest, I would be too afraid to slow down and catch a breath of fresh air. All of my life I had spent running fast before the blade. Years later, in the city, I found life to be little different. Friends and lovers would give you the ax in a heartbeat, if you were not one step ahead of them. I am always fast, running ahead of the blade, hoping that someday I will reach the end of the row, where I might sit and rest in the shade of the forest trees in the deep green refuge with only the sounds of twilight around me.

THE END

YESTERDAY I WAS HIS SON

Characters: Danny Jones, his father, Mr. Jones and Jerry

(Danny is sitting on a park bench. Two bags are on the bench beside him. He is waiting for someone)

(Mr. Jones appears left stage through an opening to the park. He sees Danny and stops for a beat, then walks with determination, showing anger as he approaches Danny.)

Mr. Jones: What in the hell do you think you are doing? Danny, your mother is worried sick about you. She said you packed and left without explaining why. We are planning to drive you to the university tomorrow morning. What are you doing here?

Danny: Dad, I'm going to college.

Mr. Jones: Like this? Without your mother and me. We have looked forward to this day. The day we would take you to the campus where all your friends and their parents will be.

Danny: I didn't think you would want to come, since I'm not going to the university.

Mr. Jones: What do you mean? Of course you're going to the university!

Danny: Dad, I'm not going to play football for you anymore.

Mr. Jones: For ME? It's what you have always wanted! That is what we have always talked about. You have a scholarship! Of course you are going to play football. You're good! It's what you want to do!

Danny: No, Dad, it's what YOU want me to do. And high school football has been fun. But Im good at other things as well.

Mr. Jones: Like art? Is that what you're talking about? (He moves Danny's bags off the bench and sits down beside him.) HE talked you in to this crap, didn't he?

Danny: I was not "talked" in to anything. It was my own decision to go to art school,—My art instructor and my counselor help me to make this decision.

Mr. Jones: Who do you think is going to pay for that? I'm not giving you a cold nickel to go to some art school!

Danny: You won't have to. My counselor helped me to get a scholarship for art school. I'm going, Dad, and you can't stop me!

Mr. Jones: When did this happen? When did you change our plans? When you met HIM! He's the reason for all this non-sense! Your mother is devastated. You're killing me here! Do you have no appreciation for all the support we've given you?

Danny: Just because I don't want what you want for me doesn't make my plans non-sense!

Mr. Jones: Art is not what you want, Danny. Football is all you have ever wanted. (He stands up with his back to Danny.) Your mother and I have waited eighteen years for this day. To see you on that university football field . . . . (He turns to face Danny) Have you lost you mind? You meet this . . . . TWIT, and he ruins everything for us.

Danny: He's an intelligent and talented guy, Dad. (Danny stands up face to face) And he has not ruined anything! He has helped to keep me from making a big mistake by helping me to realize what I really want to do with my life. What I want, Dad, not what YOU want! And you have no idea what Mom wants. You've always told her what she wants, just like you have always told me what I want. And as far as what you think about Jerry, well, that is your problem. Because HE does not have a problem. Neither do I, except for never being able to please you. Well, I'm done with trying to please you! What I want may not be important to you, but it is to me, and now is the time for you to accept that!.

Mr. Jones: You can't talk to me like that. I've always supported you in everything you've done.

Danny: No, you have always pushed me to do all that YOU wanted me to do. But no more.

Mr. Jones: (Obviously hurt and angry) Where is the son who always listened to me, took my advice, took advantage of my guidance? Where is the boy that pleased me so?

Danny: He's standing here, Dad. And I still need you. But I need for you to listen to me for once. You never gave me a chance to tell you what I want, how I feel, what I want to be! You have not been a dad. You have been a bad counselor. You've been a selfish bastard!

Mr. Jones: You can dare to talk to me this way? I've always had your best interest in mind.

Danny: Thanks for that thought, Dad, and I really think you mean it. But it's time to back off! I've made up my mind. I am going to art school! Maybe I'll be good. Maybe not. And if it is a mistake, at least I am the one who will make it. I will never be able to blame anyone except myself, and you can say, 'I told you so if I fail. But I feel good about this, partly because I am the one who made the decision . . . . without your' guidance'!

Mr. Jones: With HIS help you decided. I won't have it, you hear me!

Danny: Sure, I hear you. I always have. But you have never heard me before, and this time you have no choice.

Mr. Jones: Oh! I have a choice! I have a choice! If you go off to school with that . . . . if you give up football, you are no longer my son!

Danny: I've always listened to you, Dad. This time I actually HEARD you.

Mr. Jones: (turns abruptly and walks away. He meets a young man, Jerry, pauses for a moment to face him, then exits hurriedly.)

Jerry: (Approaching Danny) My car is over there. I'll help you with your bags. Who was that man?

Danny: I don't think I know him. But yesterday, I was his son.

(they pick up Danny's bags and exit)

THE END